What's Your Problem?

Making Sense of Social
Problems and the Policy Process

Other books you may be interested in:

Anti-racism in Social Work Practice
Edited by Angie Bartoli
ISBN 978-1-909330-13-9

Modern Mental Health: Critical Perspectives on Psychiatric Practice
Edited by Steven Walker
ISBN 978-1-909330-53-5

Positive Social Work: The Essential Toolkit for NQSWs
By Julie Adams and Angie Sheard
ISBN 978-1-909330-05-4

Evidencing CPD – A Guide to Building Your Social Work Portfolio
By Daisy Bogg and Maggie Challis
ISBN 978-1-909330-25-2

Personal Safety for Social Workers and Health Professionals
By Brian Atkins
ISBN 978-1-909330-33-7

Titles are also available in a range of electronic formats. To order please go to our website www.criticalpublishing. com or contact our distributor NBN International, 10 Thornbury Road, Plymouth PL6 7PP, telephone 01752 202301 or e-mail orders@nbninternational.com

What's Your Problem?

Making Sense of Social Problems
and the Policy Process

 Stuart Connor

First published in 2013 by Critical Publishing Ltd.

British Library Cataloguing in Publication Data
A CIP record for this book is available from the British Library

ISBN: 978-1-909330-49-8

This book is also available in the following e-book formats:

Kindle ISBN: 978-1-909330-50-4
EPUB ISBN: 978-1-909330-51-1
Adobe e-book ISBN: 978-1-909330-52-8

Cover design by Greensplash Limited
Project Management by Out of House Publishing
Typeset by Newgen Imaging Solutions
Printed and bound in Great Britain by TJ International

Critical Publishing
152 Chester Road
Northwich
CW8 4AL
www.criticalpublishing.com

MIX
Paper from
responsible sources
FSC
www.fsc.org   FSC® C013056

Contents

Meet the author

Stuart Connor

Stuart Connor is a lecturer in social policy at the University of Birmingham. His teaching and research interests include critical approaches to the analysis of contemporary social policy and practice. This work includes examining the role of governments, trade unions, NGOs, social movements and community practitioners in the fabrication of 'social problems' and attempts to legitimate and challenge particular policy responses.

Dedication

This book is dedicated to all those who doubt.

Acknowledgements

The impetus for this book came from a damp and grey day in December 2010. I was attending a demonstration in London against the increase in university tuition fees. The sounds of a thumping techno soundtrack and the sight of a pink storm trooper 'befriending' the police were long gone. I was now cold, wet and more than a little apprehensive at the sight of the mounted police forming a line across the road. I couldn't help but think: why am I here? I clearly wasn't alone in such thoughts as among all the drama and noise, heated discussions were being had as to the value of the demonstration and the goals to be achieved by such protests, debates that became more fractious as the news came through that the proposals to increase the tuition fees had been passed. What was palpable was that these were not just abstract questions, but questions that not only helped shape how people chose to act but also reflected some of the most fundamental values that people held about the world and their place within it. It is the link between such questions of where are we going, who benefits and what, if anything, should we do about it that has always made the study of policy such a vital subject to me, and that is what I wanted to reflect in this book.

Having the idea for a book is one thing, writing it is quite another. Many thanks to Di Page at Critical Publishing – your patience, comments and encouragement have been vital. I hope I can repay the faith you have put in me. I must thank my colleagues in the Institute of Applied Social Studies at the University of Birmingham. Without their support, I would not have had the opportunity to go on study leave and research and prepare this book. Special thanks go to Robert Page, Karen Rowlingson, Harriet Clarke, Tina Hearn, Sue Gilbert, Helen Harris and Pat Wright, whose encouragement and support have proved invaluable.

I have been fortunate enough to have worked with some truly remarkable and inspiring individuals. This book is the product of those experiences and the people I have worked with – I am confident that colleagues, past and present, will be able to recognise their contribution. A particular note of thanks needs to be given to Vicky Price, Graeme Simpson, Paul Grant, Richard Huggins and Richard Forster. I have learned so much from each one of you.

Writing is a lonely process, but it is not one that can be sustained without the support of others. Dad, I am not sure you realise how much you and Mom have done for me. Thanks again for all the vital lessons – up the Wolves. Hilary, your ability to cut your own path and confound expectations is a lesson for us all – thank you for everything. Finally, Eve, I have never met a finer proponent of the interrogative form. Thank you for reminding me of the value and power of a brutally simple and well-timed question. The world really is a better place with you in it.

Introduction

SO WHAT IS YOUR PROBLEM?

The aim of the book is to further deepen your understanding of social problems and your capacity to exert influence over the choices that shape related policies. The book starts from the position that you are already well versed in identifying and solving problems and that a number of the skills and resources that you have used when solving these everyday problems are equally applicable to the analysis of social problems and policies. As you read the book, you will see that the scale and levels of knowledge and influence may be different, but the questions and actions that you take in your personal life may be similar and have distinct parallels to attempts to make sense of a whole raft of local, regional, national and global issues. This is not to say that you are necessarily already fully equipped to take on the world's problems, but that your experience to date does provide an important resource and an excellent starting point for making sense of social problems and subsequent policies. For example, the reason you are reading this book may be that:

- you are on a course, possibly Social Work, Social Care, Health Studies, Social Policy, where you need to learn more about social problems and social policies in order to complete the assignment and pass the module;

- you are a tutor who wants to get some ideas about teaching a course on social problems and policy analysis;

- you have already qualified as a practitioner in social welfare and you are working with clients and attempting to address their problems (which are arguably now your problems);

- you are a 'service user', experiencing significant changes to the provision of services and benefits and you want to know more about these changes with the aim of improving the service you receive and influencing policy and practice;

o   you are a researcher, policy officer, lobbyist or advocate charged
      with completing a policy brief for your organisation and you want to
      provide an insightful and practical response;

o   you are supporting or opposing the introduction or closure of an
      initiative and want to take action on an issue in your locality, region
      or nation;

o   you want to make sense of the competing claims regarding
      problems and policies in everyday conversations, news
      broadcasts, papers, magazines and online forums and discussions
      but aren't too sure where to start.

If you consider these statements, they each represent either a
situation where a 'normal' state of affairs has been interrupted
and the goal is to re-establish and return to this normality, or,
alternatively, there is an obstacle to be overcome before an individual
is able to achieve a desired state. The notion of an interruption or
obstacle is considered an important characteristic when trying to
identify what counts as a problem. Now take a moment to consider
the list of topics in the box.

Topics

abortion, affirmative action, ageism/age discrimination, aging
population, alcoholism, animal rights, asylum seekers, benefit fraud,
binge drinking, biodiversity, birth control, birth rate, blasphemy,
bullying, burglaries, car crime, child abuse, child care (access, cost
and standard), child labour, cholera, cloning, clean drinking water
(access), credit crunch, date rape, diarrhoea, divorce, discrimination,
domestic violence, drinking and driving, drought, drug abuse/
addiction, eating disorders, education (access, cost and standard),
elder abuse, embryonic stem-cell research, pollution, euthanasia/
assisted suicide, financial exclusion, food deserts, fuel poverty,
gambling, gang violence, genetic engineering, gentrification, global
warming, gun control, GM crops, health care, hate crimes, HIV/AIDS,
happy slapping, homelessness, house repossessions/foreclosures,
human trafficking, hunger, identity theft, immigration, industrial labour
relations, inflation, influenza, inequalities, interest rates, internet
access, Islamophobia, mad cow disease, mugging, national debt,

obesity, organ and body donation, paedophilia, polio, pornography, poverty, profits squeeze, racism, rape, riots, landfill, landmines, latchkey kids, LGBT discrimination, lone parents, mental health, negative equity, overcrowding, riots, refugees, sewage and sanitation, sex trade, sexism, sexual harassment, slavery, smoking/tobacco use, speeding, strikes, suicide, stop and search, sweat shops, tax evasion, teen pregnancy, terrorism, toxic debt, tuberculosis, unemployment, vagabonds, violence on television/music videos/video games, welfare dependency

At some point or another and in some place or other, each of the topics listed in the box has been claimed as constituting a problem. That is, they have been considered to interrupt or act as an obstacle to what is taken to be a desired state of affairs. This may be clear enough when considering any one individual who is unfortunate enough to have experienced or been subject to any of these topics. But when do the problems of an individual come to be considered a social problem? Clearly not all human problems become public ones, but establishing the distinction between personal and social problems is not as clear-cut as you might think. At this point it is useful to consider the work of Wright Mills (1963), who drew a distinction between *personal troubles* and *public issues*. The suggestion was that, although an individual may experience a number of 'problems' in their life, not all of these will gain the status of a social problem – an issue that requires the public's attention or action. Wright Mills was attempting to highlight the distinction that is drawn between those problems that are 'private' (that is, to be handled by the individuals concerned) and those that are 'public' (that is, to be addressed through wider forms of social and collective action). Some of the most significant disagreements in discussions regarding social problems may centre on differences of opinion on where this line between personal and collective responsibility can and should be drawn.

If you return to the list of topics in the box, there are some that you may agree with as being worthy of being described as a social problem, others less so and some you may not have heard of.

Some problems you may claim as your own and others you may disown. On other occasions, though claiming no responsibility or ownership of the problem yourself, you still may seek to learn more, get involved and even posit solutions and offer your services. Some of us may even pursue careers that seek to help people with their problems. So, under what circumstances should any condition gain the label of a social problem (Stone, 1989)? When reviewing the list above, it is difficult to identify a common theme, apart from that they have all at some point come to the attention of a wider public. Put another way, different issues will gain public attention and support in different countries and periods. It is also the case that within a particular country and at a particular time, certain issues will gain the attention of some and not others.

Explaining these differences and changes, it may be that some of these problems simply come and go. That is, a problem is identified, policies are developed, the issue is resolved and hence the problem goes away. This suggests that the status of a social problem is dependent on the actual existence and scale of a set of objective conditions – what is described as an objectivist way of considering social problems (Best, 2008). Alternatively, and this is the position taken in this book, changes in the way that social problems are understood may be the result of differences in the way that they are constructed by policy actors. This has been described as a subjectivist or social constructionist approach to understanding social problems (Berger and Luckmann, 1967; Burr, 1995; Clarke and Cochrane, 1998), and is one that questions the value of problems and policies being seen as objective entities, open to independent scrutiny and manipulation by authorities and experts (Best, 2008; Gouldner, 1962, 1968). What such a constructivist approach also helps highlight is that claims regarding a problem tend to contain and express standards for how people should attend to the problem policy process and what are considered (un) acceptable conditions and behaviours (Stone, 1989). This is an example of what Bacchi (1999, 2009, 2012) describes as the 'what's the problem?' approach: rather than start from the assumption that social problems and the resulting policies reflect an inevitable response to pre-existing givens, attention is paid to how a 'problem' is fabricated and how a particular response to a 'problem' is legitimated and enacted (Connor, 2010). That is, claims regarding problems and policies reflect particular interests and particular perspectives on the 'right' way to do things. In this way, any consideration of your problem may also lead you to ask what are arguably fundamental questions regarding your values, your actions and your place in a wider society.

THE PROBLEM POLICY PROCESS

Making the claim that social problems are constructed is not to suggest that there is no substance behind claims regarding social problems, or that issues are imagined or arbitrary. Rather, a constructionist approach seeks to recognise the processes that inform why particular conditions should be seen as more of a problem than others, the claims and choices that are made regarding the explanations given for the cause of the problem, and what measures need to be taken and by whom. For the purposes of clarification and analysis, it is useful to consider a number of steps in what is described as the *problem policy process*, where an emphasis is placed on the notion of fabrication – that is, the combination of invention and manufacturing.

1. Fabricate the claim that a condition, set of events, or behaviour of a group of persons presents a difficulty.

2. Fabricate the claim that the condition, set of events, or behaviour of a group of persons can be changed or improved.

3. Fabricate the claim that the condition, set of events, or behaviour of a group of persons are worthy of further attention and therefore should have resources made available to address the issues that bear upon it.

4. Fabricate the explanation as to the cause(s) of the condition, set of events, or behaviour of a group of persons.

5. Fabricate the solution for addressing the condition, set of events, or behaviour of a group of persons.

Steps 1–3 represent the fabrication of claims for describing a social problem and tend to place an emphasis on establishing the scale and significance of the problem. Steps 4 and 5 refer to development of the subsequent policies, in which, when assessing the nature of the response, claims are made regarding the cause of the problem and the measures that need to be taken to address it. It is argued that claims regarding social problems and social policies are inextricably linked. This is because any characterisation of a problem also suggests that there is a solution or, more accurately, the hope that the problem can be resolved. Without the potential of a solution, it is not a problem but a condition that cannot be changed, only accommodated. Conversely, all social policies contain within them assumptions regarding the nature, scale, importance and causes of the problems they seek to end or ameliorate. For this reason, it is argued that the claims-making processes for problems and policies need to be considered together.

In an examination of this claims-making process, in addition to the work of experts, consideration needs to be given to the role and context of the everyday interactions of citizens, the debates and discussions in the media, and the interests, goals and activities of individuals, associations and social institutions. In this regard, any analysis of the problem policy process also needs to attend to the representation of social problems and policies in television, radio, newspaper and internet news reports, alongside social media and everyday discussions. This also includes attempts to understand the relationship between such discussions and the problem policy process. That is, engaging in the problem policy process needs to be understood as part of a complex and dynamic set of social relations that are subject to political, social and economic differences. Put another way, claims regarding the scale and significance of social problems are not just the preserve of expert and professional policy makers. On the contrary, this book argues that it is vital that the claims made regarding the problem policy process are scrutinised and revised by the wider public.

I'M NO EXPERT!

This is not the same as saying that experts do not have an essential role to play. Experts are experts because they have had the opportunity to devote a significant proportion of their resources to studying particular issues and questions, and clearly not everybody has the resources to develop such expertise. However, nor are experts able to become experts in all the topics that may come to be seen as social problems. More fundamentally, although the objective view that may be claimed by the expert may be deemed desirable and vital for some purposes, experts do not necessarily help a wider public consider the political and ethical aspects of the problem policy press. This places a responsibility on the wider public, or, to be more exact, publics, to perform such a scrutiny. As part of this public, you are asked not only to take time to consider your own position, but also to further develop your capacity to appreciate other people's positions and your relationship to them.

For example, recall a time when you were a 'service user'. How did you make sense of your situation? What was your priority? How did you account for your circumstances? What was your motivation? What were your assumptions regarding your capacity for action? Conversely, imagine you are the 'professional' charged with working with a service user, how might your priorities be different from those of the service user? What shapes your practice? What is your motivation? What are your assumptions regarding your capacity for action? Then again, you could be a policy officer, advocate, lobbyist or politician who is seeking to develop a set of policies to address a stated problem at a local, regional, national or even global level. In an effort to reflect the diversity of roles and relations in the problem policy process, the term *policy actor* is used to refer not only to those within appointed and formal policy positions but also to those individuals, groups and institutions engaged in the problem policy process. After looking at these issues, the book then goes on to highlight how different models and approaches foreground and draw attention to the role of particular policy actors, relations, practices and institutions within this broader conception of the problem policy process. As such, the book is written for and designed to reflect the position of a policy actor.

This take on the problem policy process suggests that attention is not just drawn to what governments do, but also needs to take account of all the institutions, relations and practices that constitute the problem policy process (Gough, 1979; Hodgson and Irving, 2007; Miliband, 1969; O'Connor, 1973; Pinker, 1971, 1979, 1992; Rose, 1981; Titmuss, 1958; Williams, 1989). This extended scope seeks to draw attention to the range and diversity of relationships and practices that create ilfare/welfare (Bryson, 1992) as well as to those institutions, relations and practices that secure and contest the resources which are then subject to distribution and in themselves constitute ilfare/welfare.

Each of these policy actors occupies a very different *position*, where position is taken to include a combination of the policy actor's world view and their location and interests within a configuration of social, political and economic relations. In this way, policy actors are considered to operate within a set of interdependent relationships, where the line between the 'private' and the 'collective' may be blurred. It is the relative opportunities and constraints for a policy actor to read, write and perform policy within these interdependent relations that is described as a policy actor's *potential*. This policy potential refers not just to an individual's ability to think about policy or their *personal resources* but also to the policy actor's location and practices within wider social, political and social relations. Thus, a policy actor's potential is realised through articulating, securing and extending their position and practices within an interdependent set of social, political and economic relations. The position of some policy actors will mean that some of these relations may operate over a greater distance than others. It may also be the case that the circle of influence of some policy actors will be greater, or at least more apparent, than others. In this regard, some policy actors may be in a position where they have more of an opportunity to realise their potential than others. However, irrespective of the reader's starting position, the aim of this book is to consider how that potential can be further developed and realised. In order to recognise and realise this potential it is necessary not only to attempt to appreciate the positions of others, but also to identify the relations that exist between the various policy actors, including your own position and relations (Walt *et al.*, 2008).

What complicates such an undertaking is that because both policy actors and relations can shift, the problem policy process should not be seen as a fixed entity. The institutions, relations and practices that constitute the problem policy process are continually being made and remade over time. Even where there is apparent inertia, work will be necessary to maintain a fixed position. Similarly, although for the purposes of exposition, a number of distinctions have been drawn between various 'steps', it should not be taken that the problem policy process follows such a sequence. That is, it should not be assumed that a problem is identified, priorities established and action proposed and then taken. Existing policies and practices may reflect particular interests and as such exhibit and realise a number of unstated or hidden assumptions as to the nature of social problems and their subsequent solutions. Therefore, the problem policy process is considered to represent a continual making and remaking of policy, through the relations and practices of policy actors at a number of different sites and positions. The position of these policy actors and their relation to the problem policy process is described through the term policy praxis.

POLICY PRAXIS

Policy praxis refers to a particular way of recognising and examining the relation between theory, policy and practice. One of the challenges for policy praxis is that there can be no prior knowledge of the right means by which a policy actor might realise an end in a particular situation, for the end is specified in and through the process of deliberating the means appropriate to a particular situation (Bernstein, 1983). Thus, policy praxis always requires and creates 'doubt'. Policy actors do not have recourse to an external authority, but instead are required to make for themselves, and with others, wise and practical judgements about how to act in a particular situation and the criteria by which acts and consequences can and should be assessed (Carr and Kemmis, 1986). Engagement with the problem policy process cannot therefore just consist of the application of abstract, timeless, classic concepts, but must involve the 'study' of particular practices and relations in specific settings.

Furthermore, this is not a form of study that is one step removed from the phenomena under investigation, but an engaged, embodied and immersed form of practice. It is this engagement and the subsequent integration of intellect and action that defines what is described in this book as policy praxis. The models and approaches highlighted throughout the book provide potential entry points for making sense of the problem policy process, but engagement with the process may well lead to a revision of these models and approaches, which in turn leads to attention being drawn to new aspects of the problem policy process, etc. Thus, policy praxis is more than action based on reflection, it challenges the distinction that is normally drawn between theory and practice. That is, it is assumed that any practice contains within it implicit or explicit theories of how to attend to the world, while, conversely, any theory is normally the result or reflection of particular practices. This has real implications for attending to the problem policy process. It is possible to start with 'theory' and other policy actors' stated aims and assumptions regarding the nature of social problems and follow these ideas through to their realisation in policy and practice. However, it is also possible to go the other way, that is, to examine a particular practice or policy and go on to reveal the assumptions, if not the interests, that it reveals. Consequently, although the book does create a sequence that takes you from reading policy through to writing and performing policy, you are under no obligation, or particularly advised, to follow this ordering. Rather, you are encouraged to 'dip' into and revisit different sections, consider the questions and potential answers raised by that section, then, most importantly, consider how the issues raised relate to other topics, approaches and models outlined elsewhere in the book and your own position and practice.

THE FORMAT OF THE BOOK

This book seeks to provide the policy actor with a number of heuristic and practical approaches to making sense of what can be a very complex and contradictory problem policy process. Drawing on the notion of policy potential, the aim is to further develop the policy actor's capacity to read (comprehend), write (create, design, produce) and perform (influence and shape) policies. Rather than learning about particular problems, the emphasis is placed on better understanding the nature of the claims that are made regarding these problems and the process that is involved in developing the subsequent policies. The book is divided into three main sections. The main aim of Section 1, Reading Policy, is to examine representations of social problems and subsequent policies and practice. For example, what are the assumptions and values evident in claims that a social condition is amenable to human action and what priority is to be given to such interventions? This section identifies and discusses the range of potential options for representing and responding to a range of social problems. This includes further examining the problem policy process, the basis of making claims and attributing responsibility (Chapter 1 – Making claims); examining the categorisation of people, objects, events and processes in the problem policy process (Chapter 2 – Equivalence and difference), and analysing attempts to persuade audiences of the legitimacy of any claims being made as part of the problem policy process (Chapter 3 – Legitimate assumptions).

The aim of the second section, Writing Policy, is to help clarify the values, interests and power relations that constitute a policy actor's position. In this respect, Section 2 seeks to provide an outline of how to answer the questions of what could/should be done and the evidence and criteria to be considered when judging the value of such proposals. This includes exploring the nature and role of policy analysis (Chapter 4 – The role of the policy analyst); a review of ethical approaches used when deciding what should be done when engaging in the problem policy process (Chapter 5 – What do you think?) and an examination of the resources and methods available for communicating a policy actor's position (Chapter 6 – Making your case – framing).

In the third and final section, Performing Policy, the main aim is to examine how it is possible to go beyond the analysis of social problems and policies and to play a part in the policy-making process. This section highlights the range of practices and activities that can be seen as part of the problem policy process, with the aim of illustrating the potential actions and criteria that can and should be employed in efforts to inform policy and 'make a difference'. An emphasis is placed on reviewing a number of models for understanding the policy process (Chapter 7 – Policy process); identifying a framework for considering the different dimensions of power (Chapter 8 – Power) and examining the range of strategies, methods and resources that have been used by individuals, groups and institutions in the struggle over the meaning and response to a range of social problems (Chapter 9 – Activities).

The book concludes by restating the argument that problems and policies do not just have an impact on people, but people can and should also have an impact on making claims regarding problems and policies (Simpson and Connor, 2011; Spicker, 2013). It may appear as if a choice needs to be made as to whether an individual should engage in the problem policy process. However, it is argued that this is not the vital question to be asked or the choice to be made. Rather, a key assumption of this book is that individuals are already involved in the problem policy process. Whether this involvement is defined and realised through an individual's role as a practitioner, taxpayer, service user or appointed policy maker, the question is not whether the individual is engaged or not, but what influence their current practices have and by what means and to what ends they should further develop their potential to engage in the problem policy process. Therefore, the book seeks not just to further your capacity to read and understand existing problems and policies, but also to support your efforts to recognise and further develop your capacity to write and perform your role in the problem policy process. The key question being: what is or should be the relationship between these two forms of activity? To this end, the book outlines the parameters and criteria by which such a relationship can and should be formed, starting with the question, what's your problem?

Section 1
Reading Policy

The main aim of this section is to examine representations of social problems and subsequent policies and practice. For example, what basis is there for defending the claim that this is a 'social problem'? What or whom is considered responsible for a social problem? What are the assumptions and values evident in claims that a social condition is amenable to human action and what priority is to be given to such interventions? This section identifies and discusses options for representing and responding to a range of social problems in order to inform an analysis and understanding of existing legitimating strategies used within the problem policy process.

Making claims

The proper course of the sage is to ask three questions. First, what things are and how they are constituted. Second, how we are related to these things. Third, what ought to be our attitude towards them.

Pyrrho of Elis (*c.*360–*c.*270 BC)

In this chapter, the question of what is a social problem is addressed. Rather than being seen as a given condition or state, what is taken to be a social problem is best described as part of an ongoing process. This is a process where a range of policy actors, individuals, groups and institutions seek to establish (a) which conditions, events and behaviours should be considered problematic and (b) why and how these problems should be addressed. The means by which the fabrication of social problems can be understood is examined. The chapter begins by examining the grounds for making the claim that this is a 'real problem'. It then discusses the question of responsibility. That is, what causes the problem and who is responsible for solving it.

THIS IS A REAL PROBLEM

When a claim is made that something is a real problem, how does the speaker know this and how is the audience able to judge the truth of such a claim (Guba, 1990)? In other words, how do we know?

First, consider a situation where people are discussing their favourite film. Person A cites Vittorio De Sica's 1948 film *The Bicycle Thieves* (*Ladri di biciclette*). Person B names *Die Hard 5: A Good Day to Die Hard*, starring Bruce Willis. As the relative merits of each film are expounded, *it's an exemplar of Italian Neorealism*, *there is an incredible car chase scene*, it may well result in a stand-off, ending with the line, *it's just my opinion*. In the absence of any established or agreed criteria by which to verify a claim, if a person thinks that their claim is true, then 'who are we' to doubt them? The logic of such a viewpoint reflects what can be described as an *epistemic relativism*, where the notion that claims can be assessed from a universal and objective standpoint is rejected (Luper, 2004). In discussions of personal tastes and preferences, we may not understand or share other people's preferences, but such differences are not problematic. But what happens when discussing the existence of social problems? Are opinions sufficient grounds for establishing levels of poverty, crime and health? Should cuts to social security be made because, in someone's opinion, recipients are abusing the system and are undeserving? Put another way, an individual's taste in films, or even their opinion as to the state of the world, does not in itself have any great bearing on other people. However, if those opinions are then considered to provide the basis for how those individuals act towards others or, in this context, the grounds for engaging in the problem policy process, then it may be necessary to identify a method and set of criteria by which claims can be justified and the circumstances identified in which policy actors would be willing to challenge and if necessary change their opinion. This is not a suggestion that people should be told what to think and not allowed to have an opinion, but to raise the expectancy that people should be able to account for and justify their position. In this regard, there is a problem with the relativist position, at least as expressed so far. Namely, how can a relativist position be considered true, when there is no way of knowing the truth? Secondly, even if it is accepted that relativism is 'valid', and what an individual takes to be true, is true, this would also include the belief that just because an individual thinks that something is true, does not make it true. But how can both these statements be true – while also holding on to the relativistic position? That is, if relativist statements are true, so objectivist accounts must also be true; this would appear to falsify the relativist claim (Pritchard, 2006).

So, it may be possible to establish that just because an individual thinks that something is a real problem, this does not make it a real problem. But this still leaves the problem of how an individual can establish whether something is a real problem or not. This is an enduring problem that can be described as the *problem of criterion* (Chisholm, 1989) – where, for the purposes of this book, in order to know that there is a real problem:

o I can only identify that I know this to be a problem, provided I already know what the criterion for knowing is;

o I can only know what the criterion for knowledge is, provided I am already able to identify instances of knowledge by which to derive the necessary criterion.

This appears to lead to a dead end. In an attempt to escape such a position, it is necessary to choose between assuming that it is possible to independently obtain the criteria for knowledge that then makes it possible to know something, or that instances of knowledge first have to be identified in order to determine the criteria. In a similar vein, there is the problem of infinite regress, that is, if every claim is reliant on the support of other beliefs and claims, then aren't those supporting claims also reliant on their support claims/beliefs, and so on and so on? Such logic may not only be annoying, but it also sits uncomfortably with everyday notions of knowing something. However, these questions do open up questions of what knowing means. So now the question has been asked as to how a claim can be justified, drawing on the work of Audi (2011), Baggini (2002), Foley (1998) and Fumerton (2006), it is time to consider some of the answers that have been given.

Foundationalism

The most common response to such a question would be that we have a basis for the claims that we make. This is described as *foundationalism* and, as the name suggests, it is a view that holds that our claims to knowledge should have a secure foundation from which to build. There are competing notions as to what these foundations should consist of. An empiricist viewpoint is that it is our experiences that provide the foundations for our claims. Therefore, any claim that something is a real problem would be judged by how well it corresponds to the experience of the world. Rationalists represent a view that it is reason that provides the basis for making claims.

The task here is to use reason in order to identify the Archimedean point, or first principles, if not self-evident truths, that can then provide the foundations for our claims. Despite the differences and historical and heated debates between those espousing the rational and empirical perspectives, what is of interest for our purposes is the shared foundationalism. The task, then, for those making claims is to demonstrate the bedrock of their claims (experiences or presuppositions) and for the audience to then adopt or reject these foundations. To many, foundationalism may sound like common sense. True, there may be ongoing discussions and differences as to what should provide the foundations for our claims, but for the foundationalist what is not in dispute is that claims require a basis.

Coherentism

Coherentism describes the approach that a claim can be justified because it fits together with other mutually supportive statements. Unlike foundationalism, the support does not come from a base. Rather the support comes from interdependence and interlocking of claims. So, for a coherentist, rather than look for the foundation of a claim, the emphasis will be placed on how a particular claim fits, relates or coheres with other claims that are held. For example, no one claim is justified on its own but only in relation to other mutually supportive claims. However, if a particular claim is not coherent with other statements that we claim to know, we should either reject that particular claim, or we need to revise the whole chain of claims as to what we know. A simple everyday example is if you know someone who you take to be a good and trustworthy friend, but then hear a rumour that they have been spreading rumours about you. These two pieces of information do not appear to fit, or at least it may not be possible to hold on to one claim while also holding the other. If you then learn that the rumour was started by someone you take to be an unreliable source, you may then dismiss the rumour, as this new information means that your claims can now cohere. That is, the rumour is false, as its origins are from an unreliable source and it is not what your good friend would do – though the possibility remains that your 'good' friend may well have made rather unflattering comments about you. It is worth noting that this notion of incoherence is not the same as the everyday use of the term, where it is taken to mean 'nonsensical'. Claims can be logical and understandable but still fail to cohere if they are considered incompatible with other claims that can be made. Coherentism can also be described as internalist, in the sense that claims about the world are judged by the extent to which they cohere with other beliefs held or claims made by a policy actor. However, this raises the question of what the relationship of these claims is to the 'external' world. Criticisms of coherentism may include that it is just a restatement of the problem of infinite regress, as at some point a hierarchy of claims needs to be made. Coherentism can also be criticised as it is possible for 'false' claims to satisfy the criterion of coherentism, though it is interesting to note how these false claims are identified.

Reliabilism

Reliabilism is an approach that argues that a claim can be justified if it is the result of a process which has been shown to provide justifiable claims in the past. This process may be the use of logic, memory or systematic approaches to the collection and reflection on experience. What counts as successful may be the ability of the process to reliably predict, describe, identify or explain events. Of course, chance, in the form of a guess, may prove to be accurate on occasions, but over time it may not be considered a reliable process. Conversely, there is also the possibility that a previously reliable process might not be accurate on this occasion. This may lead us to consider the probability of a claim being justifiable, rather than an all-or-nothing commitment/justification of a claim. It does, however, raise a fundamental objection that in some respects takes us back to the problem of criterion. How do we identify a reliable process? Don't we need a reliable process in order to support the claim that this is a reliable process? Similarly, how are we to know that the process may prove unreliable in particular instances?

Pragmatism

The tradition of *Pragmatism*, with a capital P, asserts that we can justify a claim because it 'works'. Considered a non-epistemic notion of justification, pragmatic approaches may be instrumental, in the emphasis that is placed on the ability of knowledge to enable us to act in the world, or they may be more coherent approaches that emphasise the identification of statements that fit with other statements that we may make. For example, the truth of a map may not be found in how well it corresponds with the world but in its capacity to help us get to our destination. In this regard, a claim is tested through 'trial and error' as the degree to which a claim enables successful practices and works with a wider system of statements is examined. In this respect, pragmatic approaches are relational, in the sense that, rather than seeking to identify the fixed point or rock for our beliefs, as seen in the foundational approach, the emphasis is placed on identifying the role of the statement in our actions in relation to the world. This suggests an overlap with coherentist approaches, where the evaluation of any claim regarding the scale of a particular problem and its causes may be based less on our experience of the issue, but more on the degree to which the claim fits within the system of beliefs or statements that we take to be true.

MODEST CLAIMS

This discussion does not appear to take us any closer to being able to know whether something is a real problem or not. We are left in a position where we must accept that just because we think something is a problem, doesn't make it so, while not being able to say for certain how we can know something, never mind establish what it is that we know. So where now? Well, let us assume, and this is a big assumption, that there is a truth, but that we can never be certain that we have grasped this truth. However, and this is critical, the assertion that our attempts to pursue the truth may inevitably fall short does not itself mean that this pursuit should not continue and that we should therefore accept that just because we think something is true, it actually is – quite the opposite. It really just predisposes us to the view that we need (a) to be modest and sceptical about the truth of any claims made regarding a problem and subsequent policies and (b) to be clear about the reasons we may give for our claims to approximate the truth and claim that something is a real problem.

It is useful to draw a distinction between the arbitrary and conventional. Recognising that knowledge is constructed does not mean that anything goes. Rather, it points to the fact that how we decide will inevitably reflect the conventions that have been established for what counts as knowledge. In this regard, we can both respect the conventions for establishing knowledge, while at the same time be willing to challenge and revise these conventions as and when necessary. Furthermore, as highlighted in the introduction, what becomes established as a problem is not just the result of impeccable logic or the appeal to sound evidence, but also reflects social, political and economic interests and, as such, needs to be understood as a resource to be used and an outcome of power struggles. However, as is discussed in this section, this does not preclude us from valuing and using reason and evidence to challenge and then make our own claims.

DISPUTE AND AGREEMENT

For our purposes, we are not seeking to establish one approach over another as to how we can claim to know. Rather, the reason for this distinction is to highlight the potential ways in which claims for knowledge can be made. By identifying a speaker's justification for making a claim, we are in a better position to critique that position. That is, if the speaker draws on foundationalism, we can question whether the foundation that is assumed actually counts as the self-evident truth the speaker assumes it to be. Alternatively, we can question foundationalism as an approach to justifying knowledge claims and appeal to pragmatism, reliabilism or coherentism and plausible alternatives. This may appear to be a charter for pedantry and disputation, and to some extent this is true, but in the context of attempts to engage in the problem policy process, it is important to be able to identify the nature of the dispute, with the hope of finding not only points of difference but also points of commonality. For instance, you can have two speakers who have very different forms of argument, foundationalist and pragmatist, but who still share a position regarding the conclusions they have reached regarding the scale and nature of a problem. Conversely, very different conclusions regarding the scale of a problem may have their traces in the different systems that have been used for making a claim. Finally, it may be that the differences between speakers are irreconcilable. In this instance, it may be that we have to identify a way of co-existing, rather than seeking to 'batter' the opposition into submission through claims and counter-claims.

Having looked at how we can know, attention now turns to the different claims as to what is known. The attributions of responsibility in the claims made with regard to social problems will therefore be addressed next.

WHO'S RESPONSIBLE?

Assuming we are able to arrive at a means of claiming that something is a real problem, a further question to be asked is who is responsible for the problem? An initial distinction between levels of attribution can be identified – causal and treatment (Iyengar, 1996). Causal responsibility concerns the origin of a problem, while treatment (policy) responsibility focuses on who or what has the ability to alleviate the problem. Both types of attribution are especially relevant for understanding the problem policy process. In addition to the distinction between cause and treatment, there are also types of cause and treatment, namely natural, individual and social, political and economic relations. Drawing on the insights provided by Byrne (2005) and Taylor (2003), these dimensions of attribution can be organised as shown in Table 1.1. Discussions of each of the different types of attribution are provided below.

Natural causes

A society may be presented with difficult conditions. However, it is possible that these conditions are seen as inevitable, natural and part of the human condition, unless efforts are made to persuade others that the scale and nature of the problem are both significant and issues that can be solved. That is, there may be a number of conditions

Table 1.1

An outline of different forms of attribution for social problems and subsequent policies and practices

Cause	Policy response	
	Individual	Social, political and economic relations
Natural	Fate/acceptance Adaptation Prevention Volunteer Philanthropy	Fate/acceptance Prevention Adaptation Compensation
Individual	Adaptation Volunteer Philanthropy	Education/training Surveillance Discipline Regulation
Social political and economic relations	Lobby Campaign Protest Direct action	Reform Transformation Revolution

that we face, but not all of them are seen as amenable to action. So how do we move from a tacit acceptance of the world as it is, to one where it is considered possible that a problem can be solved?

One of the most significant aspects of making claims regarding social problems is the claim that something is not a condition that we have to live with but a problem that can be solved or at least ameliorated (Stone, 1989). This involves a distinction between natural conditions that we just need to accept as they cannot be changed and problems that are considered soluble. For example, death is a problem that we must all inevitably face. However, even the most intransigent aspect of the human condition is considered a problem that can be addressed. The language of 'early or avoidable death' suggests that death may still be our ultimate fate but it is a problem that can be addressed, so that life can at least be extended to a point that we might consider a norm.

Some of the most potent historical and contemporary debates in policy are the result of disputes over the extent to which a condition is fixed or fluid. Human nature (particularly with respect to the degree to which people are selfish or altruistic), gender, ethnicity, sexuality, intelligence, if not the ordering of relationships across society as a whole (the divine order of the three estates, caste and class), have all been and continue to be subject to debates as to the extent they represent essences or states of becoming.

Assuming that it is possible that a condition isn't just something that has to be lived with, the attribution of natural causes suggests that no particular agent causes or intends to cause the problem, but that the event or circumstances are seen as inevitable. This is most evident in discussions of natural disasters or catastrophes, the supposed 'Acts of God' in insurance claims, which no one can prevent, such as an earthquake, a tidal wave, a volcanic eruption. In this context, natural may also be used as a term to cover 'accidents', where no intent can be found, but the social problem may be considered an unintended and unfortunate outcome or aberration of everyday activities.

The question of what is natural and what is an accident is a significant area of dispute when it comes to claims making. For example, to what extent could an accident have been prevented? Was the individual being reckless, or was someone else responsible? Even in the case of what appears to be the most natural event, the weather, claims and counter-claims may be made regarding the extent to which instances of 'freak weather' can be linked to global warming or whether they are just part of a natural fluctuation in the climate. In the case of the former, 'freak weather' is no longer considered 'natural' at all but is the result of human action over a period of many years, therefore opening up the scope for interventions to be made. Conversely, there are areas where claims that human actions are to be seen as 'natural', in the sense that they are unavoidable. This is most evident in situations where a whole set of relations and practices are nominalised and thereby reduced to an object or concept (Billig, 2003), for example, the economy, the market, the state, the community, the public. Once this nominalisation has occurred, the object may then be attributed characteristics, which means that it makes demands, is out of reach, out of touch, but, most significantly, is considered a given, rather than the product of human actions and relations and therefore not only made but subject to a remaking.

A common theme across natural causes is that those subject to such events and conditions are not considered responsible. In such situations they are cast as victims. This has implications for the proposed policy actions. Whether these are prevention strategies or compensation for the victims, the attribution of natural causes suggests that no one is to blame, but that someone may be responsible for responding to the results of such causes. Is the onus on the individual to prepare and respond, or is a more collective intervention required? In this respect, the claims that are made may shift from the inevitability of the condition and instead focus on the extent and impact of the event and consequences for different groups. For example, what provisions had been made to ensure the quality of buildings in areas prone to earthquake? Or could tidal-wave early-warning systems, emergency preparedness and relief-response systems have been put in place? Never mind the speed, quantity and quality of emergency services and the scope of insurance and compensation available to victims.

Individualist explanations

Individualist perspectives argue that problems can be explained through the behaviour, constituency or character of individuals (Byrne, 2005). Put another way, it is individuals that are considered responsible for the problems they experience or create. Such individualist positions can be seen as emanating from a classical liberal tradition (Welshman, 2006). Historically, individualism carries with it a radical connotation, as it emerged as a challenge to conventional feudal social ties and as a basis for resisting the encroachment of the state on the lives of individuals. In that regard, the ideas of individualism are an important part of modernity and are part of the early twenty-first-century social and cultural hegemony. For the individualist, society is or should be *networks of voluntary exchanges between autonomous individuals with their own interests and situations* (Silver, 1994, p 542).

When it comes to explaining the causes of social problems, there are variations of the individualist perspective. Attention may be drawn to the physiology of individuals, the cognitive ability of individuals, levels of knowledge, self-esteem, aspiration, behaviour, lifestyle, choices, morals or culture. These perspectives find expression in labels such as a 'culture of poverty', 'problem families', 'cycles of deprivation', where an individual's own attitude, values and behaviours are identified as the source of their poverty in a process of blaming them for their own condition (Schram, 1995; Stedman-Jones, 1984).

Consequently, in some instances, individualist perspectives may argue that the wider public is under no obligation to address the problems of these individuals, as not only should the general public not be responsible for the actions of these individuals, but any intervention may be seen as rewarding individuals for their failings. For instance, in explaining economic inequalities, an individualist perspective may suggest not only that the differences are legitimate as they reflect the work and effort of individuals but also that they are necessary to provide the sanctions and rewards that motivate individuals to continue to work hard. That is, hard work will lead to rewards and laziness should lead to failure – the hallmark of a meritocratic society. In this respect, the individualist perspective appears to be inherently anti-collectivist and the whole notion of a 'social problem' is questioned.

However, if it is argued that the problem created by these individuals creates a problem for the wider public or that intervention is required on the basis of more humanitarian grounds, then a *reluctant collectivism* (George and Wilding, 1993) may develop. Calls to monitor, survey and discipline problem populations may be made. Alternatively, help and support may be made available to individuals in order to address their deficits, possibly through a series of therapeutic interventions that seek to heal, educate, fix or empower the individual. Some of the specific measures may be very different – *do you confine a criminal or rehabilitate them?* – but the significant point is that, despite these apparent differences, the locus of the problem remains the individual. Consequently, the intervention and solution also rests with working on or with these individuals.

Social political and economic relations

This next set of explanations attempts to move beyond the individual and consider the wider social, political and economic relations as being responsible for the social problem (Byrne, 2005; Taylor, 2003). These explanations can be further divided according to whether they cite institutional or structural failure as the cause of the problem. Institutional failure refers to the absence of relevant services or the operation of institutions charged with responsibility for addressing an issue being brought into question. A structural failure explanation seeks to challenge the very nature and operation of existing social, political and economic relations (Simpson and Connor, 2011).

From an institutional failure perspective, the reforms that are suggested may be incremental or the oft-cited, by politicians at least, 'shake up' of institutions and policies. Irrespective of the rhetoric, the focus remains on the nature and operation of the institutions considered responsible. Efforts also tend to focus on government policies, the operations of statutory services or the operation and co-ordination of institutions and agencies across a mixed economy of welfare. Given this concern with amelioration – with the improvement of conditions – social administration is likely to concentrate on practical problems and solutions. The nature of the reforms proposed may be widespread and include improved training of personnel and practitioners, improved mechanisms for accountability, attempts to change the culture of organisations, improved leadership, better co-ordination, networking, partnership, competition, increased service user involvement, changes in funding mechanisms and the reallocation of resources to individuals, groups and agencies. In this regard, system failure represents a distinct reformist agenda. As noted above, the changes may be large scale and far reaching, but what is not in question is the essential soundness of the social, political and economic relations and context in which these institutions operate or the very existence of the institutions themselves, even if it is considered necessary that they take a different form. In this way, 'institutional failure' approaches can be described as non-transformational in that the institutions or governments are considered to be legitimate, but require a revision in practice.

There is a great deal that an 'institutional failure' perspective has to offer and, in historical terms at least, has achieved (Simpson and Connor, 2011). However, criticisms of the institutional failure perspective include that the institutions themselves do more harm than good (eg they take responsibility away from individuals; costs put a drain on wider economic relations; they regulate and discipline the populations they are intended to serve; or distract from or 'put a brake on' more radical solutions – transformation of social, political and economic relations). What is notable is that the criticism may be of a technical nature, where disputes are based on how the institution should be organised, or what threshold should be set for 'targeting' resources or improving decision making, responsiveness and accountability. Alternatively, dispute may centre on the actual or potential scope of action, particularly in terms of the assumption regarding who's responsible. That is, if individuals are responsible, what role do the institutions have to play? How are institutions addressing such failings or what role do the institutions have in perpetuating such failings?

Structural failure is based on the assertion that a social problem is not just an error in the operation of existing relations, but is, at best, a by-product or, at worst, the result of a deliberate intent. Structural failure attributions can take many forms. Attention may be drawn to the dominance of the state (Hayek, 1944/1991), the exploitative nature of capitalist society (Marx, 2005), the oppressive nature of patriarchal society (de Beauvoir, 1949/2010; Butler, 2004;

Firestone, 1970/2003) or hetero-normative relations (Foucault, 1988, 1990, 1992; Rich, 1980; Warner, 1991), racist, colonialist and imperialist regimes (Fanon, 1961/2004; Said, 1979; Spivak, 1988) or disabling society (Barnes, 1991; Foucault, 1971; Oliver, 1990). Such attributions suggest that it is necessary to move beyond reforms to a total transformation of societal relations. As such, structural failure explanations range from neoliberal calls for liberalisation, deregulation and the development of an enterprise culture, which seek to rewrite the relationship between the citizen and the state, through to the continuance of the class struggle (Taylor, 2003). Once again, despite the differences, attributions of structural failure suggest that since the social problem is seen to have its origins in a particular set of economic, political and social relations, it therefore follows that attempts to address it require transformation of those relations. There may be differences in what the nature of the new social, political and economic relations should be and how this transformation is to take place, but there is broader agreement on the limits of efforts to address the social problem within the existing structure. Clearly there will be many disputes between various strands of structural failure thinking, but broader criticisms tend to rest on the degree to which such positions underestimate the value and role of institutions or individuals in addressing problems.

REASONABLE DOUBT

The quote at the start of this chapter, attributed to Pyrrho, widely considered the founder of the Greek school of scepticism, reflects a fallible position, where all claims to know involve a degree of uncertainty. The chapter has sought to outline a number of very different perspectives on how we can know that something is a real social problem and who is responsible for it. Depending on how the problem is explained, certain solutions will follow. The importance of people's causal and treatment attributions for political issues has not been lost on those who are seeking to make claims. Policy actors are more than aware of the work that needs to be done to convince others that social conditions are amenable to intervention. Policy actors are also more than aware that particular forms of claims making can be an important part of efforts to gain support for their position (Stone, 1989). While it may be true that audiences are not passive cultural dupes, it is argued that it is important that people are able to further develop their potential to read and critique such claims. At this point, the emphasis is less on identifying how we should claim to know or what or who is responsible for causing and addressing social problems, but more on being able to identify the claims of others. Being able to identify the choices that have been made from the menu of options available not only reminds us that a choice is being made and why differences may exist but also provides us with a starting point for critiquing such choices.

However, notions of how we know and attribute responsibility are far from the end of the story when it comes to making claims for social problems and related policies. In order to recognise a social problem, as well as to win support and resources to address it, requires people to believe that the problem violates certain fundamental values and beliefs about how society should operate. To this end, we now move on to how categories and notions of equivalence and difference are used to show how such violations can be communicated (Chapter 2) and the role of language and imagery in persuading people that action should be taken.

2   Equivalence and difference

Who are you? When responding to such a question, you may give a range of answers, depending on the context. In a personal or informal and social setting, you may just give your name, where you come from, details of your family, job, interests and tastes. In more formal settings, such as filling out job applications or completing forms when purchasing goods or applying for loans, you may be asked to respond to certain categories. You may be asked to indicate your gender, marital status, age, educational history and qualifications, whether you are a member of any particular groups or associations, and in some instances, details regarding ethnicity, faith and disability. Whether in a formal or informal setting, you may or may not have given some thought as to why particular categories are being used and how you decide which box to tick. Are these the labels and categories that you would choose to describe yourself, or do you find yourself having to fit within existing categories? Are some of the categories natural, or do some require you to meet certain criteria before you are admitted? Are there consequences or implications for being ascribed to a particular category? Are there benefits or potential sanctions to being identified as belonging to a particular category? Why are you being asked to give such information and does this have a bearing on what information you might choose to share?

The use of categories may well be part of the fabric of everyday life, but in this chapter, questions are asked about the role of such categorisations in the claims that are made as to what is a social problem and related policy practices. In this regard, it is argued that the claims that are made about the nature of social problems and the resulting policies draw on, appeal to and help create and sustain what we may consider one of the most fundamental questions we can ask – who are you?

MAKING THE DIFFERENCE

The process of categorisation is understood as involving the equivalence and differentiation of phenomena in the representation of social problems and policies. Differentiation refers to the process by which differences and divisions are marked, whereas equivalence is the process by which similarities and sameness are signalled. Claims making and the practice of social policy involve an ongoing work of combination and separation. By examining the processes and resources that are used to establish these categories, what may be taken as the 'common sense' and natural distinctions between various people, objects and events are brought into question and open to challenge. This also helps answer the question of who may benefit from the predominance of particular categories in the representation of social problems and policies.

Categorisation can be seen as a vital part of attempts to make sense of the world. What we 'know' about the nature of the social world depends on how we organise that world and what we then choose to attend to. In this respect, categories have the potential to influence the way specific actors attend to the world and give sense to particular actions. An analysis of policy needs to consider the ways in which categories are established, sustained and managed. For example, how do ideas regarding what categories should be used change over time and how are particular categories realised in everyday policy practices? Ideas of similarity and difference are a vital part of categorisation. To create a category, you need to identify points of comparison, while also drawing distinctions between this newly formed grouping and 'other' categories. This is what Laclau and Mouffe (2001) describe in terms of the simultaneous working of two different 'logics'. That is, a logic of 'difference', which creates divisions, and a logic of 'equivalence', which creates uniformity and similarity.

Categories may be seen as reflecting natural groupings, though some categories may be more self-evident than others. In this way, the categories are seen as being 'discovered' and considered to correspond to the natural/real world. However, as noted above, the process of categorisation involves drawing distinctions and the allocation of objects, concepts or people into the respective categories. Who is responsible for these categorisations? Who decides what categories are to be used? What sets of criteria are to be established? And who meets or fails the criteria for allocating members to particular categories?

Therefore, far from emerging spontaneously from the ether, a great deal of work is involved in the creation and use of categories. As in the discussion in Chapter 1, the question is not so much whether categories are made but how do we justify the use of particular categories? Despite the wealth of research undertaken on the subject, it does not appear that the differences that exist with regard to how categories are established and which categories should be used can be addressed on the basis of evidence alone (Gans, 1995). It is not always possible to disentangle facts, values, theories and interests (Rein and Schon, 1993). The work of Murray Edelman (1977, 1988 and 1995) is particularly instructive when examining the role of categories and the synthesis of facts, values and interests in the problem policy process. With respect to the question of poverty in particular, a number of researchers (eg Boris, 2007; Chafel, 1997; Guetzkow, 2010; Handler and Hasenfeld, 1991; Katz, 1989; Larsen and Andersen, 2009; O'Connor, 2001; Schram, 1995; Simpson and Connor, 2011; Skocpol, 1988; Steensland, 2008) have examined the integration of facts, values and interests and the relationship between construction of the 'categories' and wider policy debates and practices.

SHAPING THE WORLD

Categorisation may well be a process that occurs across many levels as individuals, groups and institutions are continuously dividing and combining – (re)producing and subverting divisions and differences as part of their everyday practices. However, not all groups have the same capacity to define the categories that exist or even to define what attributions are given to a category. In this respect, the process of categorisation depends on and reflects questions of power (Edelman, 1995). Categories can be used to help shape alliances, fears and antagonisms, in a way that makes such categorisations appear to be a natural and self-evident description and response to social phenomena (Connor and Huggins, 2010).

The status of categories is therefore significant as they play a vital role in attempts to secure legitimacy for any number of practices, policies or social struggles. The legitimacy so acquired may lead others to support an action, choose to oppose an action, or believe that no action needs to be taken. Each of the categories used fabricates assumptions and claims as to what warrants membership of a particular category, the value of those within a particular category and what actions, if any, should be taken with regard to or by those in a category. In this respect, the function of categories is not to hide but to extend a particular 'truth'. In this way, there is a relationship to be determined between ways of seeing and ways of being. An assumption that underpins this chapter is that the categories we use are not self-evident, nor are they arbitrary. Rather, more often than not, they reflect purposeful choices. Thus the use of categories is not just a preliminary process in a traditional policy cycle, but part of an ongoing political process and as such should be considered integral and constitutive of the problem policy process (Daviter, 2007; Weiss, 1989).

Consequently, it is necessary to attend carefully to the use of categories as part of any claim that is made regarding the problem policy process. Unless we take time to consider the use of categories, we may fail to recognise the choices behind them and the interests that are best served by these choices. The use of categories may be an inherent part of making sense of the world and therefore inevitable, but the choice of which categories are used is not. Therefore, the presentation of these categories is not to be taken as common sense, normal, natural and self-evident, but as choices that have been made as to how and where to draw distinctions between objects, relations and groups of people. In this respect, distinctions are made and not found, and therefore the categories that inform distinctions can be revisited and if necessary redrawn. Attention to the role of categories is particularly important given the major changes in the creation and consumption of such categories in news production, politics, entertainment, advertising and everyday forms of communication. Consequently, it is argued that the role of categories in this struggle over the meaning and representation of social problems and policies is an increasingly important part of an engagement with the problem policy process.

OTHER CATEGORIES

The role of categories in understanding social problems and related policies is particularly important. Categories have the potential to help shape and influence what we take to be a social problem and how any resulting policies should be configured. Particular categories may be appealed to by policy actors in order to win support for claims regarding social problems and policies (Edelman, 1995). This is significant as particular categories tend to predominate in discussion of social problems and policies. This is particularly important in the discussion of claims making and the practice of policy, as membership of a particular category can have a number of implications as to the benefits and sanctions that one may be subject to. As noted above, membership of a grouping involves both a sense of 'belonging' and one of 'exclusivity'. What is notable in the context of debates on the nature of social problems and policies is the recurrent use of what is described as the 'other' – that is, reference to those individuals, groups and behaviours that are deemed not to belong to what is frequently an undefined 'we'.

The existence, or at least the demarcation, of what is claimed in attributions of the 'other' can be questioned, but this 'othering' is a recurrent feature of attempts to define populations and behaviours and in turn influence people's understanding of the nature of social problems and what are deemed acceptable policies (Edelman, 1977). Writers such as de Beauvoir (1949/2010) and Bauman (1991, 2004) have argued that the role of the stranger and 'otherness' is a fundamental category of human thought. This refers to the notion that no actor can establish itself without establishing a relation with an 'other'. The concept of the 'other' is most clearly evident in, though not restricted to, the construction of social categories as binary opposites, eg sane and insane, health and illness, law-abiding and criminal, expert and lay public, practitioner and service user, rich and poor.

The drawing of distinctions may not in itself be considered problematic. The identification of difference may not only be an inherent part of attempts to make sense of the world but, given the alternative, the denial of difference and imposition of uniformity, it may be recognised as a necessary and desirable practice. However, one issue with such categorisations, particularly those that seek to cast an 'otherness', is that policy actors may make repeated use of 'target group' labels. These labels, for example, can be both loaded with and bereft of meaning at the same time (Apthorpe and Gasper, 1996; Wood, 1985). Such categorisations homogenise and simplify both the alleged interests and experiences of those represented. This misrepresentation in the ascription of the 'other' can be particularly problematic given the social, political and economic context in which such 'othering' takes place. That is, historical and contemporary practices of 'othering' are found to occur in a context where the undefined 'us' category is considered normal or superior compared to the abnormal, dangerous and inferior 'other'. Similarly, what happens when you do not think that you belong to either of the categories that have been identified? Are you forced to fit, or do you need to create a category of your own? Once again, as discussed in Chapter 1, we can return to questions of whether such categorisations are reflections of the real world or ascriptions that have been made that serve the interests of those with the power to shape them. In the context of discussions regarding the claims that are made about what are social problems and acceptable policies this is a potent point, as people may be assigned to particular categories and thereby attributed with particular qualities. The 'other' may be considered the cause of social problems, the victims, deserving of further support, or undeserving and therefore worthy of further regulation and discipline.

When it comes to discussions of social problems and social policy, there is a ready-made cast of characters, including victims and villains readily available for policy actors to make use of (Edelman, 1988). Thus, a notion of 'otherness' has long been a device deployed by a range of policy actors in an attempt to garner support and generate attention for their particular issue. This may encompass a caricatured portrayal of the inhabitants and practices of another country in the lead-up to a conflict or the characterisation of political and economic elites as selfish, corrupt and reckless in an attempt to garner support for protests and direct action. Alternatively, as discussed in Chapter 1, those policy actors who seek to propagate an individualist explanation of social problems may make use of a range of familiar historical categories and labels for what may be considered a problem group – beggars, vagabonds, the indigent, spivs, scroungers, chavs, welfare queens, the underclass (Boris, 2007; Cook, 2006; Gans, 1995; Jones, 2011; Lister, 2004; Schram, 1995; Welshman, 2006).

The labels and attributes that are highlighted may change according to the time and place, but these categories provide the public with what Wright Mills (1963) called a 'vocabulary of motive' for understanding the nature of the problem. A mixture of fear, anger and disapproval is projected and cultivated, as the 'other' is shown as posing a threat to safety, cultural standards, economic position, moral values and norms. Once a distinction has been drawn, there is scope for developing antagonisms between the different groupings. This prepares the ground for the proposal of a range of interventions that, more often than not, involves efforts to address the transgression, failings and threat of the 'other'. The population as a whole is divided into those who represent a laudable and aspirational moral worth against those who seek to undermine such values and practices. It is a communication strategy that seeks to mobilise *the self-righteous and judgmental majority against those they neither know nor understand* (Jordan, 1998, p 90). In response, the policy actors making such claims will offer solutions as to how the threats and burdens posed by the 'other' can be addressed.

THEM AND US

What is interesting about these categories of 'otherness' is that while substantial efforts are made to characterise the 'other', a space is left for an ill-defined 'we' to be occupied. The 'good citizen' is brought into sharp relief by being juxtaposed and contrasted with the 'other'. On occasions, this good citizen is directly appealed to in the claims made by policy actors. The labels may vary, but hard-working families, responsible taxpayers, the squeezed middle, the silent majority are seen as being under threat or ripped off by the categories of otherness. The ill-defined 'good citizen', the 'us' as opposed to the 'them', provides a set of norms, defined by their relations to the 'other', for the good citizen to maintain and for the 'other' to aspire to. In this respect, the process of categorisation can be seen as part of a regulatory project. Although the 'other' may be most clearly subject to proposed and actual interventions, the regulatory aspects of 'othering' are not restricted to any particular 'other' that has been identified.

Simply dividing a population into categories raises a number of questions. How do you define membership of each group? What number of the population belong to the respective categories? Has the number of the respective categories risen or fallen and what is it about them (their attitudes, character and behaviour) that makes people (rather than us) become or remain a member of a particular category? As a result, not only does the membership of particular categories become the subject of investigations designed to examine their membership and 'forms of life', but the borders of such categories also become the sites of scrutiny and regulation.

The regulation may take the form of institutional monitoring, surveillance or operations. For example, if categories are produced as part of attempts to target resources, a threshold needs to be established so that it is possible to identify who does qualify for access to a service or resources and who does not. Consequently, institutions providing support increasingly become associated and arranged so that the focus is on identifying and monitoring any people deemed to belong to the target population of people needing that support. Tellingly, if the cost of providing such services comes into question, it may be that calls are made for the existing threshold for establishing access to services and resources to be revised (Connor and Huggins, 2010). Similarly, those who currently qualify through their membership of one category may be considered not to deserve such support and therefore calls may be made to raise the threshold at which receipt of services and resources is made available. The result is that, even with the best of intentions, the recipients of these services can end up being the most studied and scrutinised group in society (Schram, 1995).

However, there is also a degree of self-regulation, whereby an individual who is seeking to move from one category to another or seeking to create a distance between themselves and the 'other' may try to ensure that the correct behaviours, values and attitudes are being adopted. Those that come closest to mimicking the normative standards of behaviour are deemed most worthy of changing categories and thereby escaping the sanctions of being an 'other' and gaining access to services and resources, while those who are considered to 'deviate' most strongly from the norms of the good citizen are seen not only as peripheral or at the bottom of society's hierarchy, but also as a threat, burden and drain on the 'centre's' ability to sustain their deserved way of life.

Taken together, a combination of legislative, institutional and personal mechanisms is available to work with the 'other' and 'encourage' the 'good' citizen to perform in a virtuous manner (Clarke, 2005; Connor, 2010). In this respect, the process of categorisation is a vital part of social policy's system of rewards and sanctions that help ensure the self-regulation of individuals and institutions. It should be noted that this is not just a system that applies to individuals – it also applies to groups and institutions. The process of categorisation can be used by policy actors to reconceptualise and reconfigure relations between the state, its institutions and citizens. A vital part of these efforts is the process of categorisation and the systems of sanction and reward that follow from the distinctions that are drawn. Thus, the interdependent strategies of categorisation and the use of the archetypal 'other' need to be understood as attempts not only to justify the claims made for particular social problems, but also to reconfigure vertical and horizontal relations of power, authority and control in order to remake and enhance the self-governing capacities of institutions, communities and individuals.

The degree to which the process of categorisation can or should be avoided may be questionable. However, what can be done is to question and if necessary challenge the behaviour that should be considered ideal and the mechanisms used to sanction and reward such behaviour. The process of categorisation that appears to play such a significant role in the formation and realisation of social problems and policies should not just be seen as natural but as the result of a combination of social practices and relations. In this respect, it is necessary to acknowledge the role policies play in providing material systems of reward and sanction that ultimately address themselves to the formation of categories considered the targets of such regulatory regimes. The work of policy actors to sustain and articulate new categories and relations is never complete and needs to be continually remade. Thus, new tensions, contradictions and areas of instability are produced and these provide points of resistance and opportunities for transformation (Clarke, 2004; Daly, 2003).

DRAWING A DISTINCTION?

Categories are created through a process of establishing the equivalence and difference between different objects, people, practices, values and attitudes. The significance of examining categories when asking 'what's your problem?' is that they can help shape how people think and act as social agents. Categories do not work on their own – it is not just a question of considering the imagery and labels used to describe a particular category, although this is important. We also need to consider the social, political and economic relations and practices that are built on and help to create and sustain such categorisations. For this reason alone, the world cannot be changed just by adopting new categories and labels. However, categories can play powerfully upon established prejudices, can rationalise particular ways of explaining problems, and be used to justify resulting policies and practices. At a more fundamental level, they can also provide people with identities that, if taken as natural and common sense, help cement people in those categories and situations. This is all the more effective because the role of categorisation as part of the claims-making and policy process is not easily or readily recognised (Edelman, 1995).

Categories may be an inherent part of attempts to make sense of the world. But the question remains as to what degree the choice of a category is the product of rigorous and systematic attempts to represent the world, or the product of custom, habit, prejudice and those who seek to pursue their own interests at the expense of others (Edelman, 1988; Gramsci, 2003). As noted, this is a particularly pressing question in policy analysis, as categories do not just form part of an intellectual framework, but are both the basis and product of a number of policies and practices. It is here where categorisation as the product of policy and practice is most evident and also gives cause as to why attention needs to be paid to the categories that we use. It should also be noted that the longevity and power of any particular category is assured, not only through its propagation by those with most to gain but also by those simply looking to make sense of the world. However, rather than just seeking to help you better understand the nature and terms of these debates, the intention is that you should be part of discussions and practices that seek to influence and shape how categories could or should be produced and used.

What is notable in discussions of social problems and policies is that categories have tended to be produced and disseminated by people and institutions who would not consider themselves part of the groupings that are identified. This is clearly something to be questioned, and one response is to ensure that those depicted and assigned through a process of categorisation are involved in the assignment of those categories. At the very least, any such efforts at representation need to acknowledge that any particular category will also contain within it explicit or implicit assumptions about notions of agency, power and social relations in society as a whole. The challenge is therefore to identify and consider these assumptions and step beyond an immaculate perception (Edelman, 1995). The challenge for those producing such categories is to ensure a reflexive approach to their practice. Or, put another way, to recognise that any forms of categorisation are inexplicably linked to a politics and ethics of representation. It is here where it is argued that a critical policy analysis has a valuable part to play not only in understanding historical and contemporary debates and trends in the use of particular categorisations but also when fashioning new arguments and positions. It is hoped that you will now be in a stronger position to consider the range of categories employed by those seeking to make claims with regard to social issues.

3   Legitimate assumptions

*The right thing in speaking really is that we should be satisfied not
to annoy our hearers, without trying to delight them: we ought
in fairness to fight our case with no help beyond the bare facts:
nothing, therefore, should matter except the proof of those facts.
Still, as has been already said, other things affect the result consid-
erably, owing to the defects of our hearers. The arts of language
cannot help having a small but real importance, whatever it is we
have to expound to others: the way in which a thing is said does
affect its intelligibility.*

Aristotle, *Rhetoric*, Book 3, Part 1

In this chapter the nature and role of assumptions in the representation
of social problems and policies is examined. Policies make assumptions.
When representing a particular social issue and policy, what is stated
is part of a chain of either explicit or implicit claims about the world.
A viewer's relation to a particular representation will in part depend
on the degree to which such assumptions are shared. In this regard,
policies will both seek to demonstrate that they reflect and share the
values of those whose support is sought, while also seeking to shape
and establish a particular set of values and assumptions about the way
the world is, or at least should be, understood. This chapter examines
the strategies and resources that are used in attempts to create a
shared understanding and legitimise a particular way of seeing. This
involves examining the methods used by policy actors to legitimate
their way of making sense of social problems and their proposed
solutions. These methods are what I will describe as legitimating
practices. It is argued that the ability to recognise such legitimating
practices is an important part of reading social policy.

WHAT IS LEGITIMACY?

The notion of legitimacy refers to the degree to which we recognise
and accept answers to the question, why should we do this? Why

should we do this in this way? An influential account of legitimacy is provided by Max Weber, who describes the acceptance of an 'authority' and the requirement to obey its command. Weber also identifies three main sources of legitimacy (Weber, 1964):

○ tradition: derived from the longevity and pre-existence of societal custom and habit;

○ charisma: derived from the perceived qualities and attributes of the leader/speaker;

○ rational legal: derived from the status of authority drawing on reasonable deliberations and, in the case of political legitimacy, enshrined in laws and legal constitutions.

Legitimacy is also talked about as reflecting a benchmark or measure that needs to be met before a political institution is seen as permissible and why individuals are then required to follow the policies of such an authority, insofar as they are able to. This is not to say that if the institutions do not reach this measure of legitimacy, they are no longer able to exercise 'authority', but it does suggest that individuals are no longer expected to have to follow such policies (Rawls, 1993).

This chapter is not particularly concerned with establishing a measure of legitimacy. Neither is the aim to identify a preferred source of legitimacy. Rather the aim is to consider how legitimacy is sought in particular instances. In this regard, the discussion extends beyond questions regarding the legitimacy or otherwise of states or governments, but considers exercises of legitimacy in the discussion of policy at a number of levels: from the presentation of policies in government documents through to arguments for and against policy positions in everyday discussion and debates (Fairclough, 1989; Fairclough and Fairclough, 2012; Majone, 1989; McSwite, 1997). That is, it explores the role of legitimating practices in attempts to create a clear, positive, ethical, necessary, or otherwise acceptable action in a specific setting (van Dijk, 1998; van Leeuwen and Wodak, 1999). For the purposes of this chapter, this includes efforts to convince you why you should agree with, adopt, or at least not oppose, a particular perspective on the nature and cause of a social problem and subsequent proposals for action (Fairclough and Fairclough, 2012).

In Chapters 1 and 2 we have discussed the different categories and explanations available for making sense of society. In this chapter, an examination of legitimacy attends to the justifications of selecting particular categories and explanations. This includes a review of the various forms of legitimating practices available, with the aim of developing an appreciation of the strategies used by policy actors to legitimate policy and practices (van Dijk, 1993; van Leeuwen, 2005, 2007; Fairclough and Fairclough, 2012). An outline is provided of the language and skills developed in two related traditions, one ancient – rhetoric, the other more contemporary – critical discourse analysis.

SO WHAT IS RHETORIC?

With origins in ancient Greece, 'rhetoric' considers those aspects of communication that seek to alter the perspectives of others. One of the biggest influences on how we understand rhetoric is the ancient Greek philosopher Aristotle (*c.*384–322 BC), particularly in his *Rhetoric* (*c.*350BC/1959), where the emphasis is on being able to identify and, where necessary, use the available means to modify the perspective of another. Some of the practices, if not the labels developed by Aristotle and those who have followed in his footsteps, will be familiar to you. For example, Aristotle considered the speaker's capacity to persuade an audience to be based on how well he or she considers the interrelated elements of *telos*, *logos*, *ethos*, *pathos* and *kairos*.

○   Telos is a term that describes the particular purpose or attitude of a speech. For instance, what are the stated and unstated aims of the text? These are not necessarily the same as the aim or purpose of the subject being discussed. That is, the policy may be to introduce a new tax on wealth, whereas the aim of the speech may be to persuade you that it is in your and wider society's interests to support such a policy.

o Logos appeals to reason. Logos can also be thought of as the ability of the writer to argue his/her point. For instance, what premises and assumptions are contained in the text? What evidence, data and warrants are provided or contained in the text? What conclusions, if any, does the text make? What links are made between the premises, evidence and conclusions?

o Ethos appeals to the writer's character. Ethos attends to the credibility of the writer and his/her argument. Is the author's tone suitable for the audience and purpose? Is the diction (word choice) appropriate for the audience/purpose? How has the author attempted to establish their qualifications and their relevance to the topic being discussed?

o Pathos appeals to the emotions, beliefs and values. Pathos attends to the audience. Pathos may be heightened through the use of vivid examples, statistics, images and sounds used to engage the reader's feelings and imagination. This requires the speaker to read the values and beliefs of the audience and then identify examples that the readers relate to and care about.

o Kairos is a term that refers to the elements of a speech that acknowledge and draw support from the particular setting, time and place. That is, the time, place, and environment surrounding a moment of communication.

There is nothing inherently wrong with the use of legitimating practices. The attempt to persuade an audience of the legitimacy of the author, position and practice being discussed is not in itself a problem. The presence of legitimating practices does not invalidate the author or the message. In contrast, it is argued that all individuals will implicitly or explicitly draw on legitimating strategies as part of their everyday activities and that such practices are a necessary and desirable part of policy debates and communications. Where people occupy different positions and hold very different perspectives on the nature and extent of social problems and related policies, the candid use of legitimating practices is an important part of people's attempts to identify with each other and, most vitally, to encourage policy actors to understand things from one another's perspective (Burke, 1962). Clearly this includes attempts to persuade people of the legitimacy of a policy, but this is not considered problematic, as long as it is recognised as an act of persuasion, rather than the presentation of a self-evident truth. In this regard, whether as part of our everyday lives, or in attempts to reach consensus over global social policies, the capacity to recognise and use legitimating practices is one of the most vital skills and knowledge we can develop. Newspaper reports, transcripts of political speeches and the message boards on various webpages all provide rich source material for rehearsing the application of such skills.

It is therefore necessary to dispel, or at least reconsider, some of the widely held misconceptions regarding legitimating practices. The use of legitimating practices has, to some extent deservedly, developed a bad reputation through its association with the archetype of the politician, lawyer or salesperson attempting to persuade you of their products, case, policies or character's merits. However, it is not the legitimating practices that are problematic, but (a) the unrecognised or disguised use of legitimating practices, that is when a perspective is presented as reality, or (b) when inequalities mean that one of the actors in the relationship has a greater capacity to make use of legitimating practices than the other. In an attempt to address the former concern, the discussion of rhetoric is intended to further develop your capacity to recognise not only when legitimating practices are being used, but which particular rhetorical strategies are being employed. To address the second concern, namely, imbalances in power, it is necessary to attend to the relations between legitimating practices and broader social practices.

REVEALING ASSUMPTIONS

To date, legitimating practices have been reviewed in order to better understand how a policy actor may seek to modify the perspective of the audience. As noted above, legitimating practices can be used as part of an attempt to express oneself. However, legitimating practices are also used in attempts to impose particular ways of knowing, valuing and experiencing the world. It is therefore important to examine the role of legitimating practices in ongoing contests over the nature and meaning of social problems and policies within specific institutional and societal contexts (van Dijk, 1998; Martín Rojo and van Dijk, 1997).

Legitimating strategies can be part of a planned and systematic approach to persuading people to adopt a particular position, policy or practice. Governments and institutions have extended and intensified the use of a range of strategies and practices in an attempt to legitimise and realise particular policy projects (Franklin, 2004; Marston, 2004; Yanow, 1996). This is most evident in the British government's attempts to target benefit fraud (Connor, 2007). It is not new for an authority to attempt to propagate belief in its legitimacy (Weber, 1964) and it is argued that it is necessary and desirable for authorities to communicate information on the aims, content, rationale and potential implications of a policy. This can be seen as part of attempts to ensure the efficacy of such policies and also to help make such policies accountable. In this respect, the use of rhetoric is not considered a problem. Far from it; it should be considered an inherent and healthy part of any democratic deliberation.

However, this deliberative intent cannot be assumed. A closer engagement with the use of legitimating strategies is required to monitor and check assertions of power and knowledge. The assumption is that legitimating practices play a vital role in the creation of our reality as opposed to merely expressing it (Fischer, 2003). In this way, legitimating practices are used in the problem policy process as part of the struggle to establish particular ways of being and seeing (Fairclough and Fairclough, 2012). Therefore, by examining legitimating practices and the assumptions that they draw on, the critical reader is able to highlight how a particular author is attempting to construct versions of reality that favour their interests (Howarth, 2010).

What is being considered is the relationship between particular texts and wider social and political relations and practices (van Dijk, 1998;

Fairclough, 1989). Put another way, a policy text is a description and condensation of something that is happening in a wider social context, including a reflection of relations of power. The text will then be read and possibly performed by policy actors, though this will also be dependent on those policy actor's views and interests. Particular settings such as job interviews, advertisements, news reports, scientific journals or policy documents will contain specific conventions for what legitimating strategies are to be employed (eg Fairclough, 2003).

For example, a scientific research report will follow the format of a problem statement, hypotheses, literature review, theoretical underpinnings, sampling and method, results, analysis and discussion, conclusions and references. The ability to establish and police such rules of genre and format helps establish what is legitimate.

An examination of legitimating practices therefore requires us to go beyond a specific 'text' to make connections to past and current contexts. This is because any attempt to secure legitimacy does not stand alone. For legitimating strategies to work they need to draw on, contain and refer to assumptions: *What is said in a text is said against a background of what is unsaid, but taken as given* (Fairclough, 2003, p 40). Assumptions are not generally attributable to a specific text, but reflect implicit and explicit relations between this text and other statements and assumptions (van Leeuwen, 2007). Thus, all legitimating texts are 'dialogical' in that any claim is a link in a complexity of other claims (Bakhtin, 1986). That is, legitimating practice also refers to the wider notion of what counts as legitimate, which may or not be shared by the intended audience.

The significance of this for our purposes is that what we take to be the basis of legitimacy is, in part, shaped by social structures, such as class, status, age, ethnic identity and gender and by the specific relationships and practices that we may be engaged in and a part of. Therefore it is possible to trace back an assumption to the author's place within these social structures and practices and thereby to reveal their position, if not their interests. By bringing to the fore and then tracing these assumptions, it is possible to identify sources of power and dominance and how these sources are initiated, sustained and reconfigured within specific social, economic, political and historical relations and contexts (van Dijk, 1998).

To help with this task, Fairclough (2003), van Leeuwen and Wodak (1999) and van Leeuwen (2007) distinguished and elaborated on specific legitimating strategies.

○ Authorisation: legitimation through tradition, custom, law and individuals considered to hold authority within the existing social order.

○ Rationalisation: legitimation through the validity, efficacy and reasonableness of the claims and actions being proposed.

○ Moral evaluation: through the appeals to a value system.

○ Mythopoesis: legitimation conveyed through stories. This means producing narratives that provide lessons for the reader and audience.

Each of these broad strategies can be subdivided, where the strategy to be used depends on the setting in which the policy actor is operating. It should also be noted that all these strategies can also be used to delegitimise a position.

THE BASES OF LEGITIMACY

Authorisation – because I say so

The common theme of authorisation is that the claims made are considered self-evident. There is no suggestion that the claims should be scrutinised. There are a number of forms of authorisation: personal, expert, role model, impersonal, tradition and conformity.

○ Personal authority: legitimacy rests with the status of the individual or role, eg parent – Why? – Because I'm your mother.

○ Expert authority: legitimacy is founded on the expertise of the authority, eg Why? – Trust me, I'm an expert.

- ○ Role model authority: certain individuals, groups, institutions are to be imitated, eg Why? – Because Lady Gaga says so.

- ○ Impersonal authority: the citation of laws, rules and regulations represent what is described as impersonal authority, eg Why? – Because the law, policy, regulations say so.

- ○ Tradition: the appeal to tradition, practice, custom and habit, eg Why? – Because that is what we always do, or it is what we have always done.

- ○ Conformity: the appeal to the majority represents the authority of conformity, eg Why? – Because everyone else does, or because that's what most people do.

Where these forms of authorisation differ is in the consequences of seeking to challenge and contest them. To challenge or break a law can result in severe penalties. To disregard the advice of Lady Gaga does not yet carry such a penalty. Yet despite these differences, authorisation carries with it the notion of a hierarchical relationship, that is, that an authority knows better than the audience what is required.

Moral evaluation – it's the right healthy, normal 'natural' thing to do

Moral evaluation is based on moral values and does not rely on an imposed authority. In answer to the question, why should I do this? the answer is because it is the 'right', 'healthy', 'normal', 'natural' thing to do. This is where an action is considered legitimate because it reflects or adheres to a pre-existing set of beliefs and values. Sometimes it may not be necessary to state the full set of beliefs and values because they are considered to be 'common sense' for a particular community. In this respect, appeals to moral evaluation may be easy to spot when they are made in discussions in communities that we may consider different from our own, or, to be more specific, when we do not share the underlying beliefs and values. On these occasions, it is easy to dismiss such claims of legitimacy as being dogmatic, ideological or going against common sense. However, appeals to moral evaluation are less easy to spot when they are made to values that we may ourselves hold to be self-evident and common sense.

Being like everyone else is a value and has some overlap with the authority of conformity. However, there is a subtle difference. In the authority of conformity, the decision is being taking on your behalf (in this instance) by the majority. In moral evaluation, an individual is being asked to make a choice: be like other people. The former is a passive acceptance, in the latter the individual is expected to embrace the belief or action. This difference becomes evident when it comes to locating perceived responsibilities for actions and for securing consent.

Rationalisation – because it is reasonable

With similarities to the notion of logos discussed earlier, rationalisation tries to establish a strong or valid argument. Is the author being reasonable or asking the audience to be reasonable? As discussed in Chapter 1, the author may speak to the efficacy of a proposal, or, put another way, ask us to adopt the perspective because it works. The author may also argue that their position is legitimate because it corresponds to or is founded on a truth – an Archimedean point. Alternatively, the author may appeal to the coherence of their argument, where the argument is considered valid because it coheres with a number of other widely held assumptions or statements. This may be most clear where an author establishes or appeals to a set of principles and then establishes how their own position follows logically from the applications of such principles.

For the logic of this argument to be coherent, the reader needs to be able to recognise, if not share, the assumed premise(s). The assumed premise is often taken to be common sense and therefore does not need to be stated. For example, the common-sense view is that success (ie paid employment) is dependent on individual assets and attitudes (adaptability, hard-working, organised and a willingness to learn).

Mythopoesis – the moral of the story is...

These are moral tales, where particular characters and behaviours are shown to be rewarded or punished. Mythopoetic tales have a *persuasively evaluative* function (Fairclough, 2003, p 111). This is because mythopoetic tales not only represent examples of what people are like but also suggest how they should be (at least from the author's perspective) and therefore what the reader should aspire to (Graham, 2001; Lemke, 1995). The power of mythopoetic tales lies in their apparent self-evidence and the blurring of factual description and evaluation (Bourdieu and Wacquant, 2001).

ARE YOU CONVINCED?

Any particular attempt to modify an individual's perspective may include one or more of these legitimating strategies. However, in addition to be being able to recognise the use of these strategies, it is important to consider the assumptions that underpin them and what if anything this reveals about the position of the author. How is this done?

First, consider which particular strategy is being used. If an author tends to rely on 'authority' as a legitimating strategy, then this would suggest that he or she either assumes that this is what counts as legitimate or that the audience will believe that authorities should make the decision and can be respected, trusted or feared enough to make such decisions. This in turn reflects an assumption that the group, institution or society does and should have a hierarchical relationship.

Second, which particular form of legitimating strategy is being used? Sticking with 'authority', does the author tend to use religious forms of authority, eg religious leaders, laws or customs, to legitimate their position, or do they appeal to the authority of scientists to justify their claims? Although these two spheres of authority are not necessarily distinct, a preponderance of one or the other appears to reflect a set of assumptions about what is or should be a legitimate form of authority, either for the author or the audience. Similarly, in moral evaluation strategies, what does a particular author count as natural and therefore what does he or she assume as the norm? With respect to rationalisation, does the author or text favour the measure of 'effectiveness' in their discussions and what measure of effectiveness is used, economic growth, equality, liberty, security? Alternatively, does the author choose to foreground the importance of having principles and sticking to them, even if this comes at a cost? Finally, with respect to mythopoetic tales, what qualities are extolled (eg courage, entrepreneurship, caution, competitiveness, co-operation) and, once again, what assumptions does this reveal regarding how the world is or should be?

Attending to the use of legitimating strategies in policy debates helps make visible the way in which individuals, groups and institutions attempt to shape us and our way of seeing and being in the world. Such analyses can be undertaken at different levels and settings of the policy process. At its simplest, it is about noting that our words and actions are rarely, if ever, neutral. This is not to say that a policy actor's practices are always intended as explicit expressions of their position. Rather, a policy actor's position is realised and reflected in and through their practices and, similarly, reflects, realises and/or resists wider ideas and practices of how other policy actors could or should behave. In this respect, it is important to understand legitimacy because it goes beyond efforts to legitimate particular acts. It also has far wider social implications (van Dijk, 1998; van Leeuwen and Wodak, 1999) in that legitimating practices necessarily involve the reproduction of ideologies (van Dijk, 1998). This means that the contest over the meaning and nature of social problems and policies are also ideological struggles.

However, as noted above, what is notable in the use of legitimating practices is that in some way they are all parasitic. That is, they cannot survive in isolation, they all rely in turn on a set of further assumptions and practices. For example, personal authority relies on the individual being ascribed status in the first instance, expert and impersonal authority assumes that the process for establishing expertise and the law are in themselves legitimate; moral evaluation requires us to share the values that are being appealed to; mythopoesis expects us to learn, if not share, the lessons being taught, while rationalisation requires us to be reasonable, to share the ends that justify the means, or, at the very least, to consider the consequences above any principle. On close scrutiny, it does not take long for particular acts of legitimacy to unravel. Or, put another way, for the contingency and interdependence of legitimacy to be revealed. In this way, all forms of legitimacy require and assume a form of consent. In this respect, no use of legitimating practices involves 'one-way traffic'. While it is true that legitimating practices can involve a 'dominant' group or institution trying to legitimate their position by seeking the approval or at least acceptance from the dominated, it is, however, important to note that the 'dominated group' is not without power. It is the dominated that either willingly or resignedly legitimates the dominant group or institution (Martín Rojo and van Dijk, 1997; Vaara and Tiernari, 2008).

BEHIND THE CURTAIN

The aim of this chapter has been to help make clear the role of legitimating practices and debates in policy. The chapter has also sought to highlight the potential relations between these legitimating practices and the exercise of power (van Dijk, 1998). The aim is not necessarily to find the 'right' or true interpretation, but to 'look behind the curtain' and consider the assumptions and strategies used by the policy actor and decide whether such a position is more or less plausible or adequate as a way of seeing and being in the world (Fairclough, 2003; Wodak and Ludwig, 1999). While this chapter is primarily intended to help identify the use of legitimating strategies in policy debates, it does raise the question of why bother? Well, in the spirit of the chapter, it is possible to highlight that:

○ by learning to recognise legitimating practices in the writing of others and use them in our own, we can create texts that appeal to readers on many different levels – logos;

○ I'm a well-qualified academic and expert and I can assert with great confidence that a knowledge of legitimating strategies is an important part of policy analysis – ethos;

○   good use of legitimating practices is the mark of an intelligent
      individual, particularly with regard to the development of critical
      thinking, and as an intelligent individual, this is something that
      you will understand without me having to justify it – pathos.

In sum, an awareness of legitimating strategies will not only help a
policy actor analyse policy debates but will also inform attempts to
communicate policy ideas. For once a policy actor is able to identify
and analyse legitimating strategies, they will also be better able to
produce communications that meet the audience's needs, fit the
specific setting and convey the intended message and purpose.
However, this chapter cannot provide all the answers to the
question of what counts as a social problem or what is a legitimate
policy. Rather it is intended to identify and examine the claims that
underpin particular representations of conditions, problems and
policy solutions. The onus remains on the policy actor to consider
the concepts, beliefs and values that will guide their own actions.
Questions of what a policy actor could and should do, what sort
of society the policy actor wants to construct and maintain, and
how these ideas are best communicated are the topic of the next
section – writing policy.

Section 2
Writing Policy

The aim of this second section is to help clarify the values, interests and power relations that inform any proposed engagement with the problem policy process. Having examined the appeals and justifications used by policy actors to persuade others of their claims, the emphasis is now on identifying and exploring the range of ways that social problems can be understood and addressed. The potential roles and functions of policy analysis are considered along with the approaches available for assessing the 'goodness' of a policy actor's acts, goals and 'character'. Finally, the role of communication in the problem policy process is discussed. In this respect, Section 2 seeks to provide an account of what could or should be done and the evidence and criteria to be considered when communicating and judging the value of such proposals.

4

The role of the policy analyst

René Descartes (1596–1650) was one of the most important and influential thinkers in history. A philosopher, mathematician and scientist, René Descartes has been credited with founding analytic geometry and establishing the use of what are described as Cartesian co-ordinates and curves. As a child, Descartes was often sick and as such spent a good deal of time in his bed. This was a habit Descartes found hard to break and he continued to have lie-ins for almost all his life. It is claimed that it was during one of these lie-ins that Descartes noticed a fly crawling around on the ceiling. He watched the fly for a long time and became curious as to how it would be possible to describe the exact position of the fly on the ceiling. Such a simple question proved to be challenging. Descartes was not satisfied with saying, *to the left of*, *near* or *in the centre*, so set about plotting the position of the fly in relation to the walls of the room. That is, two lines were drawn at right angles to each other, the horizontal line was labelled X and the vertical line, Y. This created a Cartesian or co-ordinate plane, that is, two axes and four quadrants. It was now possible to plot the position of the fly by providing a location on each of these two axes – co-ordinates of (0,0). So what does this have to do with the role of a policy analyst?

WHAT IS POLICY ANALYSIS?

So far, this book has been concerned with other speakers' claims as to the nature, scale and significance of social problems and their proposed solutions. We have identified a plethora of positions, particularly with regard to 'responsibility' for these problems, the categories for making sense of social relationships, and also the different strategies available for justifying particular positions. So what response is available to this cacophony of claims making? Like Descartes' use of co-ordinates, the position to be adopted with regard to the form of policy analysis may be derived in relation to other identified positions. However, unlike Descartes' co-ordinate plane, there are no fixed positions. Instead, the potential roles for the policy analyst can be organised in relation to a number of tensions. For instance, to what degree should a policy analyst provide an analysis *of* policy or an analysis *for* policy (Gordon, Lewis and Young, 1977)? To what extent should the policy analyst provide a description of the problem policy process or seek to prescribe the relations and practices that should make up the problem policy process? Should policy analysts seek to develop theory or provide practical support to policy actors? Can and should the policy analyst produce independent, objective knowledge or is the problem policy process inherently and inevitably subjective and political (Majone, 1989)? Is the role of the policy analyst to find solutions to particular problems, or to question the agenda that has been set and to challenge the unstated assumptions that inform policy and practice (Heineman *et al.*, 2002)? In sum, when considering the role of the policy analyst, what assumptions are being made about:

○ the nature of the problem policy process;

○ the nature of knowledge;

○ how the analyst could/should engage with the problem policy process;

○ what counts as good policy analysis?

As noted already, there are a number of potential responses to the question of what is or should be the role of the policy analyst. Attention now turns to identifying three potential roles for the policy analyst, namely scholar, technician and advocate. Drawing on the work of Bulmer (1982), Greene (1990), Gubrium and Silverman (1989), Ledwith (2007), Popper (1972), Silverman (1985) and Simpson and Connor (2011), the answers each of these roles gives in response to the question 'why undertake the analysis of policy?' will be outlined.

POLICY ANALYST AS SCHOLAR

The policy analyst as scholar can best be characterised as pursuing knowledge for knowledge's sake, as represented through the caricature of the scholar in their ivory tower. In this respect, scholars position themselves as apart from the world, where they live with *the absolute freedom to pursue one's activities as one sees fit* (Denzin, 1970, p 322). The policy analyst requires a discipline, where policy is the distinct subject matter for its analysis, with the aim of producing a system of knowledge. The policy analyst as scholar seeks to go beyond common sense and discover more fundamental truths. To achieve this truth, time, space and freedom is required. Thus, policy analysts as scholars can be likened to secular clergy, analysing and ruminating over data in cloisters, content to achieve a *God's eye* view of the world (Leonard, 1996). If the scholar is accountable to anybody, it is to peers and the criterion of truth, particularly when understood in relation to the pursuit of knowledge. In this regard, the policy analyst as scholar may study policy, but only as a vehicle to informing and testing theories of policy, rather than as an explicit attempt to inform, influence or improve the policy-making process. In more tangible terms, the audience and criteria for success for the scholar will be the recognition of other scholars, if not the scholar's own conscience. In this latter respect, the scholar is considered to be driven by intrinsic factors, where the motivation is to participate in the world of ideas, discover insights and develop the capacity to collect, analyse and manipulate data and acquire a sound and valid knowledge of the world (McLennan, 2011).

What is notable is that the policy analyst as scholar is not denoted by a particular method, approach or discipline. The scholar may consider themselves to be primarily resident within a particular discipline or area of study, eg economics, political science, philosophy, history, geography, sociology, management and organisational studies, cultural studies, psychology, ethnography or discourse studies, rather than a policy analyst per se. Within and across these disciplines, scholars may employ different methods that embody sharply contrasting assumptions about the nature of knowledge and theory. At the risk of perpetuating caricatured positions, the scholar may use experimental methods and a battery of statistical forms of analysis of primary and secondary data in order to arrive at their truth. Conversely, the scholar may be defined by an interpretivist approach that seeks to identify the system of meaning-making developed and used by policy actors.

Scholar – scientist

The task of the scientific policy scholar is to develop theoretical propositions that can be generalised and contribute to a general stock of knowledge. This may involve identifying and describing what policy makers and actors do, why they do it, and what difference it makes, with the aim of providing an explanation of the causes and consequences of such policy action (Dye, 1976, p 1). Hypotheses are presented, which can then be tested using systematic and rigorous empirical research – the aim being to identify universal 'laws' that explain and predict the relationships between clearly articulated and defined variables. A scientific policy scholar's work is judged according to the degree to which the research studies that are undertaken include clearly defined, relevant and testable hypotheses, derived from theory, reliable and valid research designs and methods, and results that can support or disprove the hypothesis and as such make an original and significant contribution to knowledge (Greene, 1990).

Scholar – interpretivist

However, not all policy analysts as scholars share this 'scientist' perspective. An interpretivist tradition may place the emphasis on emic understandings, where knowledge is gained through the generation of inter-subjective meanings (Bevir and Rhodes, 2003; Fischer, 2003; Yanow, 2010) or the role of discourse in actors' practices (Howarth and Griggs, 2012; Fairclough and Fairclough, 2012; Jessop, 2009; Sum, 2009). Such interpretivist research, depending on the variation being employed, is idiographic, specific to time and place, pluralistic, divergent and contested (Greene, 1990). Values are not so much denied or stripped away, but foregrounded, if not celebrated (Smith, 1983). However, despite the ontological (questions regarding the nature of reality) and epistemological (the relations between the knower and what is knowable) differences that may exist between the different forms of scholarship, what is shared is what can be described as an academic orientation. This is where the quality of a scholar is determined by the degree to which the proper procedures of their respective traditions have been followed, their contribution to theory or the number of research articles and books appearing in distinguished journals and rated by peers.

Of course, it is possible that the findings of scholarly work can be used to inform the problem policy process, and some writers may orientate their work so that such an application is facilitated (Fairclough and Fairclough, 2012; Fischer and Gottweis, 2012; Flyvbjerg *et al.*, 2012). The policy analysis as scholar can produce the raw materials for the problem policy process. Interrogations of the concepts, definitions and measurement of phenomena may well come from the work of the policy analyst as scholar. The latest evidence and thinking may be used to rectify common misconceptions and reveal new ways of seeing and engaging in the problem policy process (Denzin, 1970). Similarly, the application of a range of statistical tests, econometrics, operations research, financial analysis, comparative methods and computer simulations, along with the documentation of policy actors' experiences and the role of discourse, semiotics and textual practices in the problem policy process, all have the potential to be adopted by policy actors in order to inform their practice. Reports, seminars and briefings, particularly as part of efforts to ensure knowledge transfer, may be used to make policy makers and practitioners aware of the latest theories and insights. For the scholar though, there is a 'categorical distinction' to be drawn between the development of scholarly work and applications of this knowledge to the problems of policy and practice (Bernstein, 1976). Analysis, application and advocacy are separate endeavours. It may be true that their theories may then be used to form policy and practice, but this is not and should not be the role of the scholar. It is for others to implement and translate the findings into practice. The scholar's attention, first and foremost, is on conducting 'good' research and developing knowledge of social problems and policy making rather than engaging in 'immediate' policy concerns or questions (Donnison, 1972; Dror, 1971; Dye, 1976; Lasswell, 1951; Sharpe, 1975).

POLICY ANALYST AS TECHNICIAN

If the policy analyst as scholar seeks to keep one step removed from the contingencies of policy and practice, the policy analyst as technician sees themselves in the service of society or, more specifically, policy makers. Policy 'makers' are no longer just a witness to the results of research, but the intended audience or co-participants. This is research and analysis for policy, rather than an analysis of policy. As such, the role of the policy analyst as technician is to proactively help policy ideas make their way into the world. The work of the analyst should have an impact, most notably to aid interaction between people in the problem policy process (Wildavsky, 1980). It may also involve anticipating issues that will need analysis; determining whether problems are real and what is causing them; defining and prioritising the goals to be achieved in addressing the problems; developing creative alternatives to address the problems; carrying out accurate and complete analyses of the impacts of alternatives, including consideration of qualitative and political factors; developing recommendations that can be implemented effectively; presenting analyses and recommendations both orally and in writing in ways that will actually influence decisions; resolving ethical dilemmas in conflicting roles; and in general, confidently applying critical-thinking skills.

In this respect, taking what Mayntz (1976) described as a normatively rational position, the technician makes use of a significant range of skills, knowledge and experience that they believe will benefit the needs of society. In what Wildavsky describes as *intellectual cogitation* joined with *social interaction* (1980, p 10), the technician revises the categorical distinction of the scholar. The technician is willing to 'get their hands dirty' and is willing to provide the necessary know-how in order to inform, if not influence, the problem policy process. It follows, then, that the policy analyst as technician can be considered to have at least two audiences – scholars and policy makers. The policy analyst may be criticised by the scholar as compromising their independence or producing transient knowledge that adds little to the wider store of enduring truths. In response, the policy analyst as technician may argue that their integrity is maintained as they are just offering 'expertise' and technical know-how to inform policy and wider society, and that this is not only able to co-exist alongside scholarship, but provides the raison d'être for such scholarship.

There are differences as to how far the policy analyst as technician's involvement with the policy process should extend. Bulmer's enlightenment model, following Janowitz (1972), sees the function of the policy analyst as enlightening the policy makers, rather than recommending or choosing particular options. Methods derived and, where appropriate, adapted from the work of the scholar enable a testing and revising of existing policy practices rather than proposing specific claims, measures or processes (Greene, 1990). The policy analyst as technician therefore has an educational function. Their role may be to develop links between theory and practice, to help policy makers interpret the significance for policy and practice of the latest evidence or concepts from the field of scholarship. More often than not, this may include considering, identifying and verifying the scale and nature of specific social problems, identifying and examining institutional capacity, documenting and evaluating policy processes and outcomes and providing conceptual fixes to enduring social problems.

Popper's (1972) engineering template augments this approach. The policy analyst not only helps identify and interpret the relevant data, but also may then make specific recommendations as to what, if any, changes can be made to the operation of policy. This may appear to move towards the realm of advocacy. However, the policy analyst as technician is not seeking to advocate their own position but to help illuminate issues, provide the information that enables others to deliberate, indicate the probability of particular outcomes, assess and evaluate the impact of practices and solve particular problems. In this regard, there is considered to be a subtle but important distinction between advocating a position and the more 'practical' and problem-solving activity of searching for the best solution from the alternatives available.

However, it is this assumed neutrality that can also lead to accusations of naivety or complicity and collaboration with regimes of power. This is a critique that is in some respects contradictory. On the one hand, the policy analyst as technician is considered to overestimate their influence. That is, rather than actually enlightening or shaping the policy process, it is more likely that they are only actually legitimating decisions that have already been made. On the other hand, by being close to the policy process, the policy analyst as technician is no longer in a position to challenge or criticise existing policy, both in terms of the assumptions held and the implementation and outcomes of particular policy practices. In this case, the policy analyst is seen either as ineffectual, at least in terms of actually shaping the policy process, or, at worst, as rationalising and legitimating exploitative and dominant policy practices (Ledwith, 2007, p 8). At heart, though, this critique can be characterised as one that does not consider that attempts to influence and shape policy are inherently problematic, but that questions should be asked as to whose interests are being served by these efforts and which direction policy is going. In sum, the technician can be described as exhibiting a policy orientation, where the quality of the policy analyst as technician is determined by the degree to which collaboration with other policy actors has been secured and the extent to which the research has informed and influenced the problem policy process. For instance, have policy suggestions been adopted? Can changes in policy and practice be traced back to the activities of the policy analyst?

POLICY ANALYST AS ADVOCATE

In response to the question of why analyse policy, the response of the policy analyst as advocate or partisan (Fink, Leonard and Reid, 1996; Harvey, 1990; Silverman, 1985) is to identify and pursue courses of action that will further a particular position, which may lead to significant changes in the relations and practices of policy (Simpson and Connor, 2011). The policy analyst as advocate argues that the goal of pursuing a particular position is a legitimate goal for policy analysis and research (Keck and Sikkink, 1998). One of the main justifications for adopting the role of policy analysis as advocate is that it just reflects and makes explicit the value-laden, subjective and political nature of the problem policy process (Gouldner, 1968). The policy analyst as advocate asserts that there is no neutral or value-free position. Even if it is possible to establish facts, it is values and interests that inform why certain facts are collected, identified and interpreted.

For instance, an advocate position may draw attention to the funding of research and the operations of agencies that, it is argued, reflect particular values and interests. This is considered to be as true of state-sponsored activities as it is for what may be the more obviously partisan position of private or charitable-funded bodies. In this respect, whether intended or not, when undertaking commissioned research and analysis, the so-called value-free technicians may find themselves reflecting and supporting the interests of those with the capacity to fund research, which may be far from synonymous with the wider public good. A stronger version of such an argument is that not only do policy analysts as scholars and technicians reflect and realise unstated assumptions and interests, but that they seek to legitimate the resulting policies and practices. That is, the claim is that policy actors make all the important policy decisions before selectively seeking the support of scholars and technicians who are willing or likely to offer legitimacy and credibility to the decisions that have already been made. In this regard, the veneer of scholarly work and expert endorsement masks what is considered to be an inherently political agenda (van Zwanenberg and Millstone, 2003). Therefore, if the problem policy process is political then policy analysis needs to take account of this politics and be willing and able to operate in such a context (Lens, 2005). Put another way, the question is not whether policy analysts should take a position, as it is considered that they inevitably will, but rather whose position does a policy analyst represent (Becker, 1967)?

It should also be noted that, although the policy analyst as advocate does not in itself represent a particular political tradition, a quick scan of job adverts will reveal the range of positions for policy analysts across the political spectrum and in a diverse number of state, private and third-sector institutions. The analyst may advocate a particular policy process, group or outcome. The advocate will make use of a range of skills, analytical tools and strategies to analyse and understand the problem policy process and further a position. This may involve promoting a particular perspective with senior government ministers or policy makers, developing communication strategies and running campaigns, lobbying and networking with other policy actors, fundraising, developing awareness of the position with the general public, orchestrating protests and building alliances, networks and coalitions with those with a shared position in an attempt to directly influence and shape the problem policy process (Alinsky, 1946, 1971; Barnes and Prior, 2009; Beck and Purcell, 2013; The Free Association, 2011; Miller and Dinan, 2008). Across these methods, though, the policy analyst as advocate's goal may be not just to inform policy actors but to explain a social problem in such a way that it becomes itself the catalyst which leads to the actions being taken to pursue the stated position.

The activist will examine the existing policy relations and practices but, rather than assume that these are the product of independent and objective research, or that these policies serve the public good, the question will also be asked, who benefits? However, the policy analyst as advocate does not seek only to identify whose interests are being reflected and realised in the problem policy process (arguably this remains the preserve of scholarship, albeit a critical form of scholarship). The policy analyst as advocate will also ask whether the existing social, political and economic relations further their stated position, and if not, what opportunities or constraints are available for furthering such a position (Gal and Weiss-Fal, 2013). As such, there is not simply an integration of theory and practice but an explicit attempt to include and foreground the position of the policy analyst in relation to the problem policy process. However, an acknowledgement of power and values is not unique to the policy analyst as advocate. Both the scholar and the technician are aware of the role of values, interest and power (post-Weber, the commitment to value-free science can itself be taken as a value position). The difference is that the scholar attempts to extricate themselves from values, interest and power, normally through calls to academic freedom and the curbing of efforts to interfere and intervene in the practices of academics, and the technician attempts to enlighten systems of power, while seeking to maintain an impartial position.

A DISTINCT ROLE?

To conclude, policy analysis can be viewed as potentially assuming a number of different roles, with each role making different assumptions about the nature of the problem policy process, the nature of knowledge, how the analyst could or should engage with the problem policy process and what counts as good policy analysis (Crawshaw, 2008; de Leeuw *et al.*, 2008; Greene, 1990; McKay, 2011; Spicker, 2011). So what is the response to the choices available? Should each of these be seen as incommensurable, should each role be ranked, where higher status is given to one over the other, or do they just accentuate different aspects of the potential role? That is, could all these roles be fulfilled by a particular policy actor at different times and places in the problem policy process. In fact, all the roles are considered essential, as different lessons and insights can be offered by each. Scholars may well learn to revise or change some of their assumptions and theories regarding the nature and role of policy making in light of the experiences and impact of technicians and advocates. Conversely, not only the evidence, but also the concepts and theories generated by the scholar will be of value to the technicians and advocates as they seek to make sense of their own practices. So, despite the differences and tensions that arise between these different roles, they can be seen as interdependent and mutually supportive. However, these practices do not operate in isolation. More often than not, some institutional support is required, even if this is of a relatively informal nature (eg networks and community), to sustain these activities. It is here that imbalances can be created, not just in terms of what roles are undertaken (a move towards more technical activity in universities as opposed to scholarship?) but also what kind of topics and activities are funded. Governments may be able to fund impact studies and evaluations, but services users do not have the same resources, and even where such work appears to address such issues, there is still the question of who sets the agenda.

In a similar vein, it should not be taken that the role can be chosen like picking a product off a supermarket shelf. A position, that is a combination of the assumptions and values that are held and the material interests and relations, will have a bearing on the role of policy analyst that is adopted. For example, a student on a course may well be offered a good degree of academic freedom, but consideration will still need to be given to the specific learning outcomes that have been established, the literature that has been recommended and the particular disciplinary approach that has been taken, in order to gain a view on what is to be expected in the analysis of the policy, eg demonstration of rigorous methods rather than impact. Alternatively, an individual may be employed to undertake a policy analysis by an organisation. In this context, consideration would need to be given to the remit that has been provided and the position of the institution. For example, is the organisation one that values providing independent and impartial analyses of policy, or does it have a stated aim of campaigning and advocating a particular position?

It will also be necessary to scan the horizon of the current nature of the problem policy process in order to arrive at an answer to the question of what form of policy analysis is to be adopted. What is notable is that the knowledge and skills of policy analysts are not only employed in what can be termed as the more formal and discrete instances of policy analysis, but also in the reading, analysis and development of the position from which such a policy analysis can take place. So, having discussed the potential roles to be adopted and how this choice is both a reflection and a realisation of a policy actor's position in regard to the problem policy process, discussion moves from what can be done, to the question of what should be done.

5

What do you think?

Thought experiment I

Imagine that you are on a reality/game show in the near future. The increased number of television and digital channels has led to increased competition to attract attention and gain viewers. The show, called *Dilemma*, puts you in the following real-life situation. In all these scenarios, after the event, should you survive, you will be given a change of identity so that no one will know what you have done and there will also be no legal consequences of your actions.

You are standing on a bridge. Beneath you, a runaway tram is hurtling down a track. In its path are five people who will definitely be killed by the tram unless it is stopped. The only way of stopping the tram and saving the people is to jump off the bridge into the tram's path.

You will be killed, but the five people will survive. Do you jump?

However, as you are about to make your decision, the show's host steps in and changes the scenario. You are still standing on a bridge. Beneath you, a runaway tram is hurtling down a track. In its path are five people who will definitely be killed by the tram unless it is stopped. This time, the only way of stopping the tram is for you, as a bystander, to flip a switch that will divert the tram onto another track. It will still kill one person, but the other five people will survive. Should you flip the switch?

Once again, as you are about to make your decision, the host steps in and makes another change. The scenario is repeated. The tram is still out of control, with five people in its path. You are back on the bridge, but now there is man standing on the very edge of the bridge next to you. You realise that with very little physical effort, you could push him off the bridge into the path of the tram. He would undoubtedly die, but he would also stop the tram from crashing into the five people, saving their lives. Do you push him?

This is not a format for a game show, not yet, anyway, but actually a thought experiment – an exercise of the imagination that can be used to examine a range of questions, including questions of morality and ethics. For example, did you provide different answers in each of the different scenarios? Did you choose to act in any of these scenarios, or do you think it is unacceptable to kill other people, even it saves more people's lives? If you did act, did you find it easier to flip the switch than to push the man next to you? If so, why? Did you choose to jump and sacrifice your own life? If not, why is your life more valuable than others'?

ETHICS

The terms ethics is derived from the Greek word *ethos*, which we discussed in the context of rhetoric in Chapter 3. Ethics can refer to the customs, habits, character or disposition of an individual, community institution or society. However, ethics is also taken to mean what is good, and how we decide what is good, for individuals and society – part of what is described as moral philosophy. It is these questions of how we should live and act that are of interest in this chapter. This may include arriving at prescriptions or methods for establishing what should be our rights and responsibilities and how to recognise what is right and what is wrong. Of course, when it comes to such ethical questions, religion, cultural traditions, professional associations, laws or the values of parents, friends and community may provide the answers to these questions. However, an examination of ethics allows us to investigate the assumptions that underpin any inherited notions of what is right and wrong. Ethics also allows us to consider how we are to act if we seek to go beyond such habits and customs.

Ethics doesn't always show the right answer to a moral problem. Indeed, it may be that there is no one right answer as to what ought to be done. However, a rudimentary understanding of different approaches to ethics does provide a map and set of navigational tools for exploring such debates. In this chapter, you are being asked to consider, not just what your own ethics are, but also what status and role do ethical statements have in your world view. For example, do you think that there are ethical 'facts' and therefore your role could or should be to identify these facts and to ensure that people are aware of and then abide by these ethical truths. Alternatively, do you think that ethics is subjective, and your role is to clarify your own ethical position and explore the reasons for this position, while also attending to the ethical positions of others? Now consider the implications of these two different positions for policy. As a moral realist, you may argue that the means and ends of a particular policy are wrong and therefore it should not be permitted. The point being that once the truth is established, there is little room for discussion. Policy becomes the preserve of authorities who are able to decide the nature of these ethical truths. Alternatively, moral subjectivism means that we can never be certain of the ethical goodness of our policies. We also have to take into account the potential myriad of perspectives on what counts as an ethical policy, which also may require us to leave open the possibility that our own view of ethics can be revised, particularly as we have now introduced some doubt as to what is right and wrong.

The approach from moral realism appears to leave little room for debate, while moral subjectivism can lead to a cacophony of dispute and disagreement, with no apparent criteria or mechanism by which to resolve such disputes. Arguably, this is where policy comes in again, for not only may a policy be intended to do good, but the process of policy making also has the potential to provide a forum for exploring, examining and challenging what is the good to be sought in the first instance. This is part of the role of the analysts, as discussed in Chapter 4, but is also an issue to be described further in Chapter 7. For the moment, though, this chapter is concerned with identifying the potential terms of such a discussion and the different approaches available for deriving ethics and what counts as the qualities of goodness that are to be realised. To this end, three approaches, namely consequentialist, deontological and virtue ethics, are outlined and summarised in Table 5.1. These three approaches do not exhaust all the potential ways of examining ethics, and this overview should not be considered as providing a comprehensive account of each. Rather the aim is to draw attention to some of the key features, assumptions and implications of these ethical approaches for engaging with the problem policy process.

Table 5.1

An outline comparing virtue, consequential and deontological approaches to ethics

	Virtue	Consequentialism	Deontology
Description	An action is judged 'right' if it is what a virtuous actor would do in the same situation, eg the development of habits that reflect and realise what it is to 'live well' (eudemonia)	An action is judged 'right' if it promotes the best results, eg maximises utility	An action is judged 'right' if it adheres to an a priori rule, principle or duty, eg categorical imperative
Orientation	Ethic of character – what characterises the person, institution and society we should be?	Ethic of conduct – what sort of acts should we engage in to create the best results?	Ethic of conduct – what sort of acts should we engage in that reflect what we take to be right?
Influential writer	Aristotle (c.340 BC) Alasdair MacIntyre (2007)	Jeremy Bentham (1789) John Stuart Mill (1861)	Immanuel Kant (1781, 1785, 1788)

CONSEQUENTIALIST ETHICS

In essence, consequentialism, or results-based ethics, can be summarised as describing those approaches that argue that what makes an action good or bad depends on the results of that action – that is, the assessment of consequence. In this respect, consequentialism can be seen as drawing on two principles.

○   The rightness or wrongness of an act depends on the consequences of that act.

○   The more good results an act produces, particularly when compared to its alternatives, the better or more ethical the act.

From this perspective, when faced with a dilemma, an actor is expected to consider *which action will maximise the positive consequences?* This form of instrumental reasoning, where focus is on establishing the best or optimum means for meeting a stated end, clearly provides a useful starting point for identifying what is the right act, but, as is the case with all these ethical approaches, it raises as many questions as it answers. This explains the variants of consequentialism. For example, a distinction can be drawn between act and rule consequentialism. In act consequentialism, an assessment of the consequences is applied to every single act. This is considered to offer flexibility, but is also time consuming and demanding for the actor. Rule consequentialism, which is considered the more practical and efficient approach, places the emphasis on what ethical rules can be derived from the consequences of particular acts (eg it is wrong to lie, because individual acts of lying have led to bad consequences). Other questions raised by a consequentialist approach, particularly in the context of understanding the problem policy process, is what counts as positive (and to whom) and what it is that should be maximised. Should the actor seek only to maximise their own pleasure (hedonism) or should they seek to maximise the happiness of the majority, while also minimising the unhappiness of the minority (utilitarianism)? However, one of the most interesting aspects of consequentialism is the argument that intentions, methods and character are far less important; it is the results that matter. In this respect, no particular act is considered unethical, as it is the consequences that are the measures of 'goodness'. For instance, this is why the consequentialist can justify the use of murder and torture, as they will argue that it is the consequences of these acts that should be considered, not the act.

DEONTOLOGICAL ETHICS

Deontological ethics (also described as non-consequentialist, duty-based ethics, from the Greek *deon* for duty, obligation, necessity) or Kantian ethics (named after its most famous proponent), attends to what people do, rather than the results or consequences of their actions (Baron, Pettit and Slote, 1997). In contrast to the instrumental reasoning of consequentialism, a substantive form of rationality informs deontological approaches (Herman, 1993). In more everyday language, when people say *but it's the principle* or *doing the right thing* or declare, *it is just wrong*, they are most likely invoking a deontological approach to ethics and behaviour. That is, they are describing an act that appears to transgress their values and beliefs. In this respect, a deontological ethics seeks to make explicit and agree the duties and principles by which people should act (eg Kant's categorical imperative, discussed below). Therefore, once these duties have been established, to be ethical is to adhere to these duties.

One way of expressing this approach is to consider the deontologist living according to a set of moral laws (eg it is wrong to torture). What is of note is that the resulting laws may end up being similar to the rules developed by rule consequentialism. However, the difference lies in the reason for abiding by these rules. For the deontologist, it is not because of the consequences of torture that you should not do it, but because it is the wrong thing to do, even if it could be argued that in this instance the act might have positive consequences for many (eg the use of torture provides information that could be used to prevent a bombing and save many hundreds of lives). In this respect, a deontological approach offers the actor a degree of certitude. No longer is there a need to make an assessment of the likely consequences of an act, as the concern is with the action itself. So if an actor knows that a certain action is good, then they should do it, irrespective of the consequences for themselves or anyone else. Similarly, if an act is deemed to be bad, they should not do it, even if there are beneficial outcomes for themselves and others. The major challenge for the deontologist is in knowing what the duties to be enacted are and, if necessary, living with the consequences of their actions. So how do we know a moral act from an immoral one? What are the duties and principles to be enacted and how are they to be identified? In contrast to the consequentialist, where an empirical approach is taken to assessing the consequences, a deontologist makes use of 'reason' to identify the necessary duties.

Kant is the writer most responsible for espousing a deontological ethics. Kant sought to base an ethics on a 'categorical imperative' – a rule for all the other rules that would be true in all circumstances. Kant's categorical imperative can be expressed in two ways, though it is important to note that these are seen as reinforcing each other, rather than as two distinct rules.

1. If you want a moral rule to be enacted, you should also be willing for it to become a general law. That is, everyone else should do the same in the same situation. Put another way, there cannot be one rule (or exceptions) for you and one rule (or exceptions) for others.

2. Moral rules must respect human beings. This refers to the principle that all human beings should be treated as free and equal, and as such, be treated as ends in themselves, not as objects to be used when realising your own ends. For example, it would be unethical to bully or deceive a person to get what you want.

It would be wrong to caricature deontology as simply a rule-bound ethics. Deontology does not mean adhering to any and all laws, but only to what have been identified as moral laws. This can bring deontologists into conflict with state-enacted laws.

Furthermore, motives and intention are important. For example, if you adhere to a principle because you believe it is your duty and the right thing to do, this would be considered ethical, at least from a deontological perspective. However, if you adhere to your duty for some other reason, for example, you are worried about the consequences for yourself or are seeking to gain by being seen as doing your duty, then your actions could no longer be seen as being ethical. Similarly, if the discharging of your duty was as much the result of accident as a purposeful act, then you cannot gain credit for this, at least not in terms of ethics. In sum, deontological ethics is doing the right thing, for the right reason, because it is the right thing to do.

VIRTUE ETHICS

A number of writers have called for a revaluation of the potential of virtue ethics for informing the problem policy process (Banks, 2012; Banks and Gallagher, 2009; Clark, 2000; McBeath and Webb, 2002; Rhodes, 1986). Virtue ethics is most closely associated with the works of Plato (*c.*427 BC) and Aristotle's two ethical treatises, *Nicomachean Ethics* and *Eudemian Ethics*, and the discussion of character in his *Politics* (see Bostock, 2000), as well as the more recent work of MacIntyre (2007). Virtue ethics attends to questions of character and what traits embody and realise a good life and society. That is, rather than attend to questions of the consequences of action or duties, the most vital questions are what sort of person or society one should be (Vardy and Grosch, 1999) and what characteristics a person or a society needs in order to flourish – eudemonia?

When defending or proposing an action, the virtue ethicist will not make a primary appeal to principles or results but to the idea of what habits realise and reflect what counts as a good person or society. In this respect, the right act is taken to mean what a virtuous person would do given the same circumstances. For example, policies for the poor are provided, not because of the results that will be produced, or because it follows from *a priori* principles, but

because you want to be or live in a society that develops policies that
seek to eradicate poverty (Banks, 2012; Hugman, 2005).

Virtues are generally considered to be 'acquired' human qualities
that can be revealed and developed as part of the fabric of one's
life and reasoning (MacIntyre 2007). A fundamental question then
becomes: what are the virtues that are to be realised in one's life?
For example, a traditional list of cardinal virtues includes qualities
such as prudence, fortitude, temperance and justice. It then follows
that the way to build the 'good' society is to help people to recognise
and nurture these values, rather than resort to sanctions and
rewards to encourage or deter good and bad practices.

However, it may be considered to go against the grain of virtue ethics
to identify cardinal virtues that need to be followed, or to identify
a fixed set of procedures for identifying and developing particular
virtues. Therefore, rather than debate the virtue of these virtues,
it is the oft-neglected question of how these virtues are identified
and developed that is of interest (Houston, 2003). To this end, an
emphasis tends to be placed on identifying practices and sensibilities
that are conducive to a nurturing of virtue at an individual and
societal level. For instance, virtues can be developed and nurtured
through practical reasoning (MacIntyre, 2007), experience, reflection
and circumspection (McBeath and Webb, 2002) or consensus
building through deliberation and reflection within a group
(Houston, 2003). This deliberation and reflection may consider
questions such as, who am I? Who ought I to become? And how
ought I to get there? (MacIntyre, 2007). A variation of such a project
that has particular relevance to social research and the problem
policy process is that of *phronesis* (Flyvbjerg 2001; Flyvbjerg *et al.*,
2012; Spicker, 2011).

Variously translated as practical judgement, practical wisdom,
common sense, prudence or the art of judgement, phronesis is an
approach to the study of social phenomena based on a contemporary
interpretation of work by Aristotle. Contrasted with forms of
knowledge such as *techne* – know-how (technology/technician) and
episteme – analytical, scientific knowledge (epistemology/theory/

academic), phronesis involves making explicit values and interests
when assessing the possibilities, problems and risks faced in specific
domains of social action. It does not seek to provide a truth that
needs to be complied with, show the consequences of an action,
or identify a universal set of principles that need to be followed.
Echoing MacIntyre (2007), the principal task for the phronetic policy
analyst is to clarify the values, interests and power relations as a
basis for praxis. The point of departure for such research can be
summarised in four value-rational questions, which researchers ask
and answer for specific problematics in their fields of interest, for
instance, in policy and in practice.

○ Where are we going?

○ Who gains and who loses, and by which mechanisms of power?

○ Is this development desirable?

○ What, if anything, should we do about it?

The 'we' referred to in the first and last of these questions refers
to those researchers asking the questions and those who share
the concerns of the researchers, possibly including people in the
community or organisation under study. Thus the 'we' will always be
situated in relation to a specific context. The third question is clearly
normative. Phronetic researchers are highly aware of the importance
of context and perspective and see no neutral ground, no 'view from
nowhere', for their work. Question two, the power question, is what
distinguishes, in particular, contemporary from classical phronesis.
It is a basic tenet of phronetic research that insofar as social and
political situations become clear, they get clarified by detailed stories
of who is doing what to whom. Such clarifications provide a main
link to praxis.

Phronesis does not take what is considered 'good' as a given but
seeks to reflect on and consider what counts as good and how this
can be achieved as part of its inquiries. What is less clear is the
degree to which those undertaking phronetic policy analysis seek to
realise their own position or the position of those about or for whom
the research is undertaken, or a combination or accommodation

between the two. In this latter respect, phronesis, particularly in contemporary versions, takes as a given that there will be a plurality of interests, and therefore that one of the issues that needs to be recognised is whether and how such different positions can co-exist. As noted above, this does not just involve an intellectual accommodation of different positions, but an examination of the different positions in relation to questions of power. Hence, a main task of phronetic research is to provide in-depth narratives of how power works and with what consequences, and to suggest how power might be changed and work with other consequences.

The primary purpose of phronetic social science is not to develop theory per se, but to contribute to society's practical rationality in elucidating where we are, where we want to go, and what is desirable, according to diverse sets of values and interests. That is, rather than be determined by an external authority or set of procedures, decisions are made in the manner of a virtuoso social actor. Thus, phronesis is about providing the type of knowledge that can be used to inform decisions in the absence of absolutes – by combining a concern with what is possible with questions of what is desirable and for whom. As such, the goal of the phronetic approach is to add to society's capacity for value-rational deliberation and action.

SO WHICH OF THESE ETHICAL APPROACHES IS ETHICAL?

All of these approaches can be subject to criticism and these criticisms may be both practical and theoretical (Baron, Pettit and Slote, 2008; Fitzpatrick, 2008). For consequentialism, how are we to know the consequences of an act? Because, by definition, the consequences follow the act, does this mean that we cannot confirm the ethical nature of our actions until after the event, or, more likely, are we appealing to the probability of the results of our actions? How confident can we be that an act is related to the consequence? When it comes to measuring happiness, well-being, satisfaction, pleasure and utility, how are these measured? Over what period of time should the consequence of an act be considered, short, medium or long term? In the context of policy, can the policy actors making the assessment be considered neutral and informed inquirers, or are they considering the consequences for particular groups? In sum, although it would seem to be desirable to pursue acts that increase what we count as 'good', and consequentialism allows us to research and hence review what this 'goodness' should entail, it is far from a straightforward task. This is particularly the case for an individual actor seeking to apply a consequential assessment to each of their acts. It is, however, a task that could be undertaken through the capacity and resources available within the problem policy process. However, for those who believe that the intent, methods and character of the policy process need to be considered, deontological approaches may have more appeal. Deontology may offer some certainty, but it also has a strong potential for being absolutist. To what degree can a duty be considered to be universal? Do people need to accept these duties or are they just accepted by individual actors? Virtue-based approaches, apart from the difficulties of agreeing on what the virtues are, do not necessarily provide clear guidance on how to act in particular situations. Arguments from virtue theory can appear tautological. That is, what makes something ethical is that it is the act of a virtuous person, but a virtuous person is one who exhibits virtuous acts. However, this apparent tautology is considered to reflect the necessary generative and reflexive aspects of virtue approaches. That is, what counts as virtuous is not something than can be identified by abstract reasoning alone, or through empirical research that reveals the consequences of one's actions, but through a continuous and reflective engagement with the world.

So far, though, we have only discussed what counts as a good act or policy and the theories of how we can arrive at such answers. Attention now turns to the question of what is the desired destination of these acts. What are the principles that we should live by and strive for in society? What are the desirable outcomes by which we assess the consequence of our actions, and what are the virtues to be exhibited in individuals and society as a whole?

Thought experiment II

Imagine that you are given the opportunity to decide what society you can live in and you are given a choice of three.

Option A is a society where the individual's civil and political liberties are cherished. There is a level of freedom of expression, religion, association and protest. In essence, people are given the freedom to choose the lifestyle they want to live. In society A there are also high levels of crime, both property theft and crimes against the person. Finally, society A is characterised by high levels of wealth and income inequality, ie 10 per cent of the population owns 90 per cent of the wealth.

Option B is a society where there is very little emphasis placed on individual civil and political rights. A number of lifestyles are proscribed and there is a strong intolerance of any faith except that permitted by the state. Public protests are not permitted. Incidences of property theft and crime against the person are low, but those who are considered to transgress the laws that have been established are subject to severe punishment. Income levels are good and income and wealth levels are relatively equal, though a minority have low incomes, at least when compared to society A, ie 95 per cent of the population has access to 99.5 per cent of the wealth; 5 per cent has access to 0.5 per cent of the wealth.

Option C is a society where the individual's civil and political liberties are cherished. There is a level of freedom of expression, religion, association and protest. In essence, people are given the freedom to choose the lifestyle they want to live. In this respect, it shares the characteristics of society A. In society C, however, property theft and crimes against the person are not quite as high as in society A, but significantly higher than in society B. With respect to income and wealth, the country is egalitarian. Income and wealth levels are lower than those found in society B, and are equal to the levels of wealth and income exhibited by the bottom 10 per cent in society A.

The question is: which society would you choose? What are the reasons for your choice and what does your choice of society reflect about what is important to you and what you think constitutes a good society? Is it possible to agree that any one of these societies is better than the others? If so, what criteria are to be used when making such an assessment? Are the values that your preferred society exhibits of more importance to you than the standard of living? If so, what values are the most important? Which values are you willing to forego in order to secure a good standard of living for you (and for others)? What other pieces of information would you like to have about the respective societies before making your choice and how would these pieces of information influence your decision making and why? Would your answer change if you knew in advance what position you would take in the respective societies? Or would your decision change if you had no prior knowledge of who you would be, as in Rawls' (1999) use of the *veil of ignorance*?

LIBERTY, SECURITY AND EQUALITY

When it comes to answering questions about what is the good society and therefore what social policies we should be working towards, three values tend to be invoked – liberty, security and equality.

Liberty

Berlin (1969) drew a distinction between negative and positive liberty. Negative liberty is taken to mean the absence of constraints from others, most notably external authorities. This is frequently expressed as individuals and groups seeking freedom from the intervention/interference of the state and related institutions, eg freedom to travel, free speech, free press, freedom of faith and no restrictions on smoking and drinking. Positive forms of liberty refer to the capacity of people to pursue their chosen ends. In this regard, a negative form of liberty may be necessary but insufficient for people to be free to pursue their ends. For example, you may be free to travel, but you may not be able to afford the cost or have access to the means by which to travel. Therefore a positive view of liberty may lead to calls to ensure that people have access to the necessary resources in order to enact their freedoms. In this regard, positive forms of liberty begin to resemble aspects of equality (see below). Proponents of negative liberty may oppose the redistributive policies necessary to secure such positive notions of liberty, as this may lead to greater interventions by the state in people's affairs (Hayek, 1944, 1960). The concept of deservingness and how the rewards accrued by individuals and institutions reflect the efforts and choices they have made is more likely to be part of discussion of policies and negative liberty. More broadly, the debate between the merits or otherwise of positive and negative liberty is a reflection of a fundamental question regarding liberty, that is, the co-existence and compatibility of individual freedom with the freedom of the many.

Security

At its simplest, security refers to an individual or state being free from harm and the threat of harm. As a value in policy debates, it is closely associated, though not synonymous, with the notion of order. In this regard, security can be taken to mean protecting lives and 'ways of life' – that is, maintaining traditional patterns of social relationships. A society may establish authorities to maintain this security and order. The concept of risk and individuals' and institutions' capacity to read, manage and respond to risk is more likely to be part of discussion of policies that value security (Kemshall, 2002). Most obviously, this may include the military institutions to protect a nation state from external threats, or the institutions and agents of the criminal justice system. However, there are also a number of regulatory authorities that seek to protect the public from harm, for example, health and safety authorities and bodies that seek to regulate the activities of the pharmaceutical, food, financial, manufacturing and service industries. Professional bodies and inspectorates in medicine, education, law and social care help prevent and respond to any instance of harm, trades unions have the remit of providing security for their members, and the system of social security, as the name suggests, traditionally at least, has the function of providing a secure income for those times when people are unable to secure their own incomes. Finally, what is the role of the ideological state apparatus (Althusser, 1971) in ensuring the order and security of society?

Clearly, there will be significant differences of opinion over what levels of security it is possible and desirable to achieve, the nature and accountability of the institutions responsible for security and what are to be considered acceptable ways of doing things with respect to the preservation of social order. That is, if a society exhibits a range of social, political and economic inequalities, is the maintenance of such an order to be considered desirable?

Equality

Once again, equality can exhibit a number of variations. First, historically at least, distinctions have been drawn between equality in terms of political and civic rights (see below) and what have been described as social, economic and welfare rights (Marshall, 1967). Debates can focus on what should be a right once a civic and political right has been established, should every citizen have access to those rights? In discussions of social and welfare policy, questions of equality tend to focus on social and economic factors. Social equality can refer to everyone having an equal opportunity to access services to secure the resources for their welfare (equality of opportunity) or ensuring that as any inequalities arise, measures are taken to redistribute and equalise the outcomes (Fitzpatrick, 2005). With the former, the pursuit of social equality may well be considered satisfied even when inequalities exist, as long as an equal opportunity to secure welfare has been made available to all or their needs have been met. However, the possibility that equality of opportunity may lead to unequal outcomes, with some not able to meet their social needs, may require further measures in order to create equal outcomes (Gough and Doyal, 1991).

THE VALUE OF VALUES

There will be differences over what each of these 'values' means, their relative desirability and the degree to which they are incommensurable. For instance, efforts to secure equality of outcome may be considered to impinge on notions of negative liberty. Similarly, attempts to maintain security may impinge on notions of liberty and, depending on the existing social arrangements, prove an obstacle to securing equality. Alternatively, proponents of equality of outcome may argue that it not only meets the criteria of equality, but also those of security and positive notions of liberty. Historical and contemporary political and policy practices have sought to secure, or on occasions limit, the expression of these values in the form of rights and responsibilities of the state and its citizens. Thus, at different times and in different states, some rights and responsibilities have gained precedence over others. This raises the question of whether a universal set of human rights is desirable, and if so, what rights are to be included and pursued. For example, take a look at the civic, political and social rights below. Do you think some of these rights are more important than others? Does the list need to be extended or reduced? Can each of the rights stand alone, or are they mutually exclusive or interdependent and mutually reinforcing?

Civic, legal and political rights include:

○ the right to life;

○ freedom from torture;

○ access to fair trial;

○ freedom to assemble and associate;

○ freedom of thought, religion and expression;

○ the right to privacy;

○ the right to participate directly or indirectly in the establishment or administration of government, eg to vote in and stand as candidates in elections.

What have been described as social, economic and welfare rights cover a number of domains:

○ the right to work, the right to a free choice of work, and the right to good working conditions;

○ the right to strike and the right to form and join trades unions;

○ the right to social security, health and education;

- ○ the right to an appropriate standard of living (eg food, housing and sanitation);

- ○ the right to cultural identity and the right to take part in cultural life.

In sum, this is only the briefest glimpse into the debates about the nature of these values and principles, never mind the critiques of each of the positions and the means by which they are to be achieved. However, for our purposes, this brief outline does help us identify the types of values that may be appealed to in the problem policy process and when it comes to writing policies, and what type of society we would like to create. For example, what combination of these values is to be considered acceptable and desirable? It may not be possible to achieve each of these values in its pure state, ie total liberty, security, equality. However, in the context of engaging in the problem policy process, it is useful to consider what direction society or particular policies are going in, eg is society becoming freer, more equal or more secure?

THE POLITICS OF ETHICS

The farfetched moral dilemma provided at the beginning of the chapter is a variation of the 'Trolley Bus' thought experiment discussed by Sandel (2010) in his introduction to his discussions on the question of justice. In terms of arriving at and securing what is understood as ethical and a reflection of social justice, it is possible to overstate the degree to which ethics informs people's everyday practice, never mind deliberation in the problem policy process. That is, it is not clear whether it is possible to identify and agree on what is good in order for policy actors to be able to use such criteria when choosing their actions and evaluating their practices. For a start, each of these approaches tends to draw attention to slightly different types of ethical question. For example, virtue ethics is concerned with what is a good, noble, admirable or virtuous individual or society, while consequentialism is more concerned with identifying what counts as a good act (Baron, Pettit and Slote, 1997; Gray, 2010). Furthermore, people may fall short of such ethical standards, either because they behave 'irrationally' or because circumstances mean that it is not possible to maintain the moral standards prescribed by others. Of course, there is also the particularly thorny issue of whether it is possible or desirable to establish one set of criteria for what counts as 'good', given the number of ethical approaches available. Ethics can be used by dominant groups as a source of social control. In this regard, ethics is seen as closely entwined with, if not an extension of, political ideologies that have the prime purpose of sustaining inequities in power and resources.

Once again, we have returned to questions of material circumstances, politics and power. This indicates that we may need to go beyond ethics when considering what is a good society and how it is to be realised. However, this does not mean that ethics need no longer concern us. A working knowledge of the various ethical approaches can allow us to identify where differences occur in the contests and heated debates. That is, are the differences a result of the stated ends to be achieved or, where the goals are agreed, in the nature of the methods and actions to be taken to achieve them? On a more personal level, a knowledge of these ethical approaches may help you work through what your own position is with regard to what is a good society and how to judge the value of your acts. This is considered vital to any project where you seek to identify, justify and communicate your position in the writing of policy. However, given the different approaches and criteria, it may also remind us of the contingency of our argument and that, although we may be committed to our position, a degree of doubt will remain, which opens the possibility that our own and others' positions can be redrawn.

6

Making your case – framing

Consider that you are attempting to develop people's understanding of an issue and you have the opportunity to produce a short film for uploading on to the internet or broadcast media. The topic is unemployment and you want to raise awareness of the experience of the unemployed.

Option A is that you tell the story of a young woman who is unemployed. You show her in her house, simply furnished, struggling to deal with the demands on her limited budget, talking about the number of rejection letters she has received from employers, the disheartening nature of her situation but how she still hopes to secure paid work in the near future.

Option B is that you still feature the young woman, but also go on to describe the impact of the closure of one of the area's biggest employers, the number of people who are also unemployed in the area, the increased use of food banks and payday loans, and the demands being made on local voluntary and statutory services.

Which approach would you choose and why?

The aim of this chapter is to consider the resources and methods available for making the case of what constitutes a social problem and what action is to be taken. The intention is to help readers identify resources and approaches that they can make use of in their own lives when answering the questions where are we going and is it desirable? It is about communicating to others how and why things matter. That is, what objects, values, people and relations are a particular policy actor, and potential others, prepared to act for and towards. In order to look at this, we revisit a number of the issues and strategies that were covered in Section 1 when discussing reading other policy actors' claims about the problem policy process. However, now the emphasis is on how a position can and should be communicated and justified to others. This is a critical and yet frequently neglected aspect of writing policy. To this end, following an outline of how and why communication has become an increasingly important part of the problem policy process, the use of framing by policy actors is discussed.

A CONTEXT FOR COMMUNICATION

It is argued that communication strategies have come to play an increasingly important role in the problem policy process. The increasing scale and significance of communication strategies is related to wider social, political, technological and economic changes during recent decades (Franklin, 2004; McChesney, 2007; Rai and Cottle, 2007; Thompson, 1995). Changes in the media structure include the expansion of the tabloid press and the increasing importance of television and 24-hour-news channels, which have helped create a new way of visualising politics (Fornäs, 1995; Scalmer, 2002). Particularly notable is the rise of the internet and social media spaces (van Aelst and Walgrave, 2004; Arora, 2012; Couldry and Curran, 2003; Dahlberg and Siapera, 2007). These new media spaces have made a profound change in the scope and potential for communication strategies, where 'real-time' communication with a potentially global audience can take place at relatively little cost to the user. Combined, these changes in media technologies have helped modify existing local, regional, national and global media spaces and create new ones.

Alongside such developments within the media has been the growth in numbers and subsequent competition between those making claims as part of the problem policy process. The increase in numbers has intensified competition for revenue streams (eg donations, government subsidiaries and contracts) and public attention. Consequently, there have been significant changes in the management and governance of the various institutions involved in the problem policy process (Simpson and Connor, 2011). Most notably for the purposes of this chapter, an increasingly competitive environment has created the demand for policy actors to promote themselves and account for their performance in an attempt to attract, retain and meet the expectations of supporters (Vestergaard, 2008). To this end, a range of policy actors have sought to draw upon, or at least reflect, the expertise of consultancy, advertising and communication professionals (in-house and agencies) (Franklin, 2004; Miller and Mooney, 2010). When it comes to communication strategies, at least, a blurring of the distinctions between statutory, for-profit, third sector and even social movements can be seen in the approaches taken to communicating their respective positions (Benford and Snow, 2000). Indeed, when it comes to communication, the approaches used by some social movements and the third sector, particularly those with severe resource limitations, have been cited as exemplars for the for-profit sector (Vestergaard, 2008; Wootliff and Deri, 2001)

The benefits of policy actors successfully communicating their position are numerous. Most obvious is raising awareness of the problem and the policy actor's position. This can be important when communicating directly with appointed policy actors or in attempts to consolidate and generate wider support among a wider public (Franklin, 2004). This wider support may help in the securing of funding and resources or to increase pressure on appointed policy actors and strengthen the legitimacy of the campaign and position (Gamson and Wolsfeld, 1993; Walgrave and Manssens, 2000). However, as discussed already in Section 1, claims making is a contested process. In addition to any issues with regard to articulating the policy actor's own position, there is also the myriad of competing claims to contend with and the practical question of getting your message out and understood as intended (Benford and Snow, 2000).

Communications is a term used to describe and include a range of activities, such as lobbying, spin, marketing, media and communications strategies, public affairs and public relations. A range of communication strategies and methods are available for policy actors seeking to write policy and engage in the problem policy process. Similarly, there are numerous potential sites and institutions where such communication strategies are enacted

(Miller and Mooney, 2010). Essentially, communication strategies can be used to describe an organisation's relationship with partners and clients. This can include members of the organisation, politicians, civil servants, clients, trade and business associations and groups, think tanks, trades unions and individuals and institutions in the media. Communications work seeks to engage these various audiences in order to communicate and explain the organisation's policies, provide relevant information, lobby and seek support for the organisation's aims. Communication strategies may include efforts to lobby policy actors, monitor media, manage issues and disseminate information through public relations and strategic communications advice. Communications work may either be undertaken 'in-house' for a company or 'independently' through the use of consultants. Those engaged in enacting communication strategies operate under a number of different job titles including public, parliamentary and government affairs, policy officer, government and public relations, European affairs, stakeholder relations, political and policy researchers and advisors, external affairs, information and communication officer, campaign officer and corporate affairs. As indicated above, a wealth of literature is available for examining the use of communication strategies per se, but this work tends to attend to questions regarding political communications, party politics, electoral or government news management (eg Connor, 2007, 2010; Deacon and Golding, 1994; Franklin, 2004; Hood, 1998) or focuses on issues outside the realm of social policy. In contrast, with some notable exceptions (eg Miller and Mooney, 2010), relatively little attention has been paid to the role and significance of communication strategies by a range of actors in the contemporary problem policy process. Regarding what methods are to be used and how a position is to be communicated, a range of issues need to be considered. These include institutional and relational factors, such as the capacity of the policy actor to communicate their messages, and the political, social and economic context in which the policy actor is operating, including the configuration of media and access to spaces for debate and discussion (a theme developed in Section 3). What this suggests is that communication is not just a technical process that follows on from the establishment of a position, but should also be considered integral to the problem policy process, or even a contested aspect of that process. A number of writers have highlighted the need to better understand the relationship between social relations of power, frames, discourses and the means by which these discourses are communicated and legitimated (Brah, 1996; Fairclough, 2000; Marston, 2004; Miller and Mooney, 2010). It is the concept of framing, which has already been foreshadowed in Section 1, that can be used to make sense of such efforts to write policy

THE WAY PEOPLE SEE THE WORLD

One of the most influential writers on the subject of framing, George Lakoff, describes frames as the *mental structures that shape the way we see the world* (2004: xv). In this respect, framing allows us to act efficiently and create a sense of order in what can be a complex, uncertain and fluid world. Rather than have to make sense of every new experience from afresh, frames drawn from previous experiences create an expectancy, which is then confirmed by these 'new' experiences as they conform to our expectancy. This does raise the question, though, of the extent to which we see what is there or what we expect or want to be there. The important point is that, once a message is recognised as being familiar, and has found its place within previous experiences, people no longer need or tend to process the rest of the information. This is the essence of framing, presenting new information in terms that people are already familiar with and understand. This can make framing appear to be a conservative endeavour, as once a frame is established any new information tends to be understood with reference to it. In theory, when a frame 'fails' in a particular context, it may be replaced by an alternative frame. However, when there is a disjuncture between the facts and the frame, it is more likely that the facts will be rejected or revised rather than the frame.

Opportunities for reframing are made available, though, as it is assumed that people are capable of and tend to use different sets of frames in different settings. For instance, people may make sense of family relations using one frame but consider the workplace using a different frame (Lakoff, 2004). The challenge for the policy actor, then, is to ensure that the right frame is used when communicating their position. This is a significant challenge given the further assumption that people do not only reason and react to material circumstances out of self-interest but also with regard to their values. This combination is what has been described in this book as people's positions. Here position does not refer to a person's nominal identities in terms of membership of groups or institutions, but what these identities and groupings reflect of that person's notions of freedom, justice, security, faith, reason and solidarity. So when a frame works, it is because it offers cues that enable the audience to recognise the issue as reflecting their position. So a frame isn't simply a slogan repeated over and over; rather, it should be considered akin to the fabrication of a map that not only helps people to organise and represent the world but to operate within it. Hence, framing is more than the use of sound bites, slogans or memes but is an embroidering of people's everyday sense making.

IN THE FRAME

In its most literal sense, framing refers to the boundary that we put around an image. Deciding where to put the frame, and in turn altering the composition of the image, can change the way the viewer understands the image. An instructive example of the influence of this framing is provided by Saul (2009). Saul provides an account of John Hilliard's (1974) series of photographs, Cause of Death. The series includes four photographs; each photograph contains the image of a body, where the majority of the figure, including the head, is covered with a shroud. This may lead us to assume that the body is dead. Each of the four photographs is framed differently. The first image is shown next to some rocks and is titled 'Crushed'. The second image is shown at the edge of some water and is titled 'Drowned'. The third image is shown next to a fire and its title is 'Burned'. Finally, the fourth image is at the foot of an edifice, possibly a bridge, and is titled 'Fell'. Depending on the title and composition of the image and the associations we make between the elements included, we may reach different conclusions as to how the subject might have died. The significant point is that the body is in the same location in each of the four images, the only difference being which aspects of the wider shot, that includes all the elements, Hilliard chose to include within the frame. Thus, by simply changing the frame and repositioning the subject at the top or the bottom, the left or the right of the wider frame, we are able to change how the picture is read. The use of framing, particularly in the context of the problem policy process, extends beyond this rather literal example. But the figurative use of framing holds because a particular frame helps specify what is included and excluded from consideration (Apthorpe and Gasper, 1996). Framing makes some features more salient than others in the problem policy process. In this way, framing predisposes a viewer to consider an event, fact, relation or institution in a particular way (Kuypers, 2009). Reflecting the dynamics of the problem policy process as a whole, frames help define problems, identify causes, provide moral judgements and propose remedies (Kuypers, 2009). As seen in Section 1, this may include the attribution of responsibility and which categories are brought to the fore and what groups remain hidden from view (Apthorpe and Gasper, 1996).

THE STRUGGLE FOR MEANING

If this notion of framing is adopted, its significance and importance for the problem policy process quickly becomes apparent. If frames shape the way policy actors see the world, these frames will also influence what counts as important, what goals are to be pursued, what counts as a good action and outcome and why, and how the audience should be involved (Benford and Snow, 2000; Gamson, 1992). As described above, frames help reflect and realise a policy actor's position. It follows, then, that if a policy actor is able to understand and shape the frames that are used to understand the problem policy process they also have the potential to shape the problem policy process as a whole. Consequently, efforts at (re) framing, that is, attempts to provide triggers for particular frames, are a vital part of efforts to establish a position and shape how the problem policy process is to be understood (Lakoff, 2004).

As there is potentially a great deal to be gained if amorphous issues can be framed in a particular way (Rein and Schon, 1993), there is intense competition over what is to be taken as the preferred, if not the correct, frame for understanding the problem policy process (Larsen and Andersen, 2009). Policy actors, news media and various forms of popular culture all frame stories in a way that may predispose the audience to draw particular conclusions with regard to the claims being made (Brewer and Gross, 2005; Nelson, Clawson and Oxley, 1997). Frames not only draw attention to particular aspects of a problem or a way of understanding the rationale for a policy, they also reflect and realise particular positions that encourage the audience to respond in a particular way (Entman, 2004). One of the reasons that such an emphasis has been placed on reading policy in Section 1 is that the framing of social problems, particularly in broadcast, print and digital media, helps establish *habits of thought and expectation* that, when repeated, can have a strong influence on how 'new' information is processed. In these particular struggles for representation, a range of resources and strategies are available in order to secure a particular way of seeing (Frameworks Institute, n.d.). Béland (2005) highlights the role played by *policy entrepreneurs* and their use of frames as important weapons in mobilising and securing support for specific positions and proposals. These frames help political actors to 'sell' their policy to the public. Similarly, Baumgartner and Jones's (1993) theory of *punctuated equilibrium* has been used to document the efforts of policy actors to punctuate and achieve rapid upheavals in established policy areas (Robinson, 2004).

USING FRAMES

Activating frames in part involves being clear on the position that is to be communicated and the frame to be employed and then identifying cues which will ensure that this position is both familiar and understood within the desired frame. For instance, imagine that a policy actor is asked to advocate or oppose the Tea Party Movement (TPM) that has recently entered the political scene in the USA. If advocating for the TPM, a policy actor may seek to present it as being made up of and therefore representing the everyday American frustrated with fiscal and federal policies and practices, which, despite being a grass-roots movement, has been able to demonstrate a real impact on the traditional political parties and operation in Washington. Alternatively, a policy actor who is opposed to the TPM may seek to frame it as outside of the mainstream, representing an incoherent amalgamation of grievances, sometimes unpalatable, if not extreme, positions, that is merely a flash in the pan, and which, despite appearances, is actually supported by and affiliated to establishment interests (Boykoff and Laschever, 2011). Alternatively, a policy actor may be required to develop a case for supporting a public-funded early-years childcare service. How should support for childcare policies be framed? Should it be seen within the context of poverty programmes? Is access to affordable and quality childcare a women's rights issue, or should it be framed as a fundamental part of children's education and development (Palley, 2012)? Alternatively, are policies that seek to ensure affordable and quality childcare to be understood as part of labour market policies and attempts to make work pay?

In both these examples, the significant point is that a number of potential frames are available for understanding an issue and each of these frames will reflect and realise the frames and position of a particular audience. Those policy actors who seek to communicate their position can make a choice of whether to operate within these frames or seek to break them and establish a new frame. However, Lakoff (2004) identifies a strong note of caution. If seeking to contest an alternative frame, policy actors should ensure that it is not cited and then negated. The reason for this being that negating a frame only serves to evoke it, which then serves to reinforce it. For example, with reference to the TPM example above, if defending the Tea Party against its critics, it would not be advisable to begin by stating that the movement does not represent an incoherent amalgamation of grievances that is merely a flash in the pan, because, even if the advocate goes on to establish reasons for defending such an assertion, the frame that the Tea Party is a flash in the pan and does not possess a coherent programme or agenda has already been evoked and, according to Lakoff (2004), reinforced.

FRAMING THE STORY

Another way to think about framing is to consider the story being told. More often than not, the claims that are made about the problem policy process can be considered to follow the structure of a simple story. They define a problem, explain how it comes about, and show what needs to be done to avoid threats or improve circumstances. A historic example of such framing is highlighted in Adam Curtis's *The Century of the Self*, a four-part documentary series produced for BBC television in 2002. The documentary highlights the work of Edward Bernays in the 1920s. Bernays was funded by a tobacco company in the USA to help end a taboo against women smoking. Bernays set out to establish a connection between smoking cigarettes and the idea of challenging male power. In order to make such a connection, Bernays staged an event at New York's Easter Day parade. A group of rich debutantes were persuaded to hide cigarettes under their clothes and, at a given signal during the parade, were to remove and light up these cigarettes. Meanwhile, Bernays informed the press that he had heard that a group of suffragettes was preparing to stage a protest by lighting up what they called 'torches of freedom'. The event drew a great deal of press and industry attention. The documentary discussed how Bernays' 'torches of freedom' provided an example of how an image could be created to develop an awareness of a topic, event, product or policy, and to shift people's orientation to an issue and potentially lead to changes in behaviour.

Finally, another aspect of framing is illustrated through the two scenarios for telling the story of unemployment provided at the beginning of the chapter. Option A can be described as an episodic frame. Even if the individual is shown in a 'sympathetic' light, normally taken as adhering to the norms of the audience, the focus on the individual reinforces a more individualistic explanation. In contrast, Option B can be described as a thematic frame, where, alongside identification with the individual, the context is also highlighted and the young woman's capacity to act on these institutional and structural factors is shown to be limited. Therefore, it is suggesting, if things are to change, other agencies and institutions need to be involved.

Now consider a further option, option C. A young unemployed woman is depicted. In addition to looking for work, the young woman is also shown working as a member of a local coalition against poverty, organising a campaign against recent social security reforms. She is shown to be a member of a social media network and responding to the potential eviction of another member of the coalition. She is then shown at the relevant address with other members of the coalition against poverty. The numbers blocking the door mean that the bailiffs are unable to continue with the planned eviction of the tenants. In this third scenario, a different story is being told to that found in scenario A. What form of action is being illustrated in scenario C when compared to A? Who may be supportive/antagonistic to the position being illustrated here and why?

In sum, it is argued that these different forms of framing processes have an impact not only on how people make sense of information, but also on what people choose to attend to, the decisions they support, reject and make. Consequently, in the context of writing policy, an understanding of frames is particularly valuable. That is, for a policy actor's communication to be successful, it is necessary not just to have an understanding of framing, but also to understand the frames of competing policy actors and those of the intended audiences.

INFORMATION OR PROPAGANDA?

Proponents of strategic framing argue that the judicious use of frames, both in terms of identifying the frames of an audience and contesting and subverting the frames of competing claims making, is a vital part of the problem policy process. If framing is as fundamental to people's everyday practices as has been suggested, then it may not be possible to avoid an engagement with framing or even to recognise particular instances of framing. This is not necessarily because framing is a particularly erudite activity only available to a privileged few – far from it. As framing is part of everyday practices, it is one activity that everyone can and does partake in. It is framing's immediacy and proximity which means that it can remain hidden in plain sight. Therefore attention to the use of framing not only makes these everyday and purposeful framings more explicit, it also provides a starting point for developing policy actors' potential to use framing when writing policy.

The challenge for those engaged in framing is to consider the difference between instances when framing is being used to facilitate effective communication and when framing is akin to propaganda (Fischer, 2003). There is no quick or easy answer to this dilemma. Do policy actors need to identify some criteria of truth by which to assess the use of frames or do they need to contend with some sort of discursive will to power, as competing policy actors do battle for our hearts and minds? Policy actors may well attempt to make their claims regarding the policy process appear obvious. Language and imagery is chosen that suggests that the claims being made are inescapable and little, if any, room is left for refutation (Apthorpe and Gasper, 1996). Similarly, the potency of frames can come from their ability to simplify complex policy issues and processes. However, this simplicity can also lead to a failure to attend to the complexity, uncertainty and open-ended nature of the problem policy process. Therefore, rather than seeking to make positions appear obvious and unquestionable, a more reflexive view of framing may acknowledge the contingency and particularity of the position and then seek to establish the relevance and potential that such a position offers the audience. As such, a reflexive use of framing assumes and arguably relies on a deliberative form of the problem policy process (Dryzek, 2000).

In some respects, this question brings us back to issues of how we justify our claims and our position. The contingency of a position does not mean that anything goes or license a form of nihilism where nothing matters. It does, however, suggest that when making decisions about how to engage in the problem policy process, there is no external authority that can be drawn upon in place of the policy actor's own choices. Therefore, policy actors are required to take responsibility for the choices that are made, if not the circumstances in which they find themselves. This includes how policy actors choose to shape society, the type of society that they are seeking to create and how such a society is realised. However, what happens if policy actors do not agree with how people could or should live? In a context where we seek to ensure that a plurality of positions can co-exist, it may be considered vital that frames are used reflexively, so that the position of the messenger and the basis of such claims are made clear. Put another way, framing becomes problematic when it is no longer seen as a frame but is taken as common sense or the truth. There is a responsibility on the reader to be able to recognise and consider the role of frames in the way they make sense of the world and the claims that people make with regard to the problem policy process.

The focus on the struggle over meaning and the role of framing in the problem policy process is not to suggest that all policy issues should be turned into textual matters. Foregrounding 'communication' in this way is not intended to suggest that language, images and ideas are more important than material practices and relations. On the contrary, following Miller and Mooney (2010), it is argued that communication strategies are not separable from the wider strategies of policy actors and as such represent a vital aspect and expression of political agency. Attending to the contested nature of meaning, at least in this instance, is not intended to be done at the expense of science, rationality and a concern with material relations, but rather at the expense of restricted articulations of science, reason and deterministic approaches in human affairs (Dryzek, 2000). It is about drawing attention to the struggle between individuals, interest groups, social movements and institutions over the framing of social issues (Wenden, 2005). It is in this struggle and the fashioning of new arguments and positions in the problem policy process that framing and the potential to read and write policy is most vital.

Section 3
Performing Policy

The main aim of this section is to examine how it is possible to go beyond the analysis of social problems and policies and to play a part in the policy-making process. A number of models for understanding the problem policy process are outlined, namely the expert model, the deliberative model and the crisis model of policy 'making'. The assumptions regarding the nature of policy making and what are regarded as the key relations, processes and actors in each of these models are discussed. Alongside these models, different dimensions of power are discussed, where the emphasis is placed on identifying the assumptions that inform each of the dimensions of power and the implications for those policy actors seeking to develop their potential to perform policy. Last is a consideration of the relationship between taking action and the position of the policy actor reflected and realised through efforts to perform policy.

7   **Policy process**

*One must lie low, no matter how much it went against the grain,
and try to understand that this great organization remained, so
to speak, in a state of delicate balance, and that if someone took
it upon himself to alter the dispositions of things around him, he
ran the risk of losing his footing and falling to destruction, while
the organization would simply right itself by some compensat-
ing reaction in another part of its machinery – since everything
interlocked – and remain unchanged, unless, indeed, which was
very probable, it became still more rigid, more vigilant, severer, and
more ruthless*

Franz Kafka, *The Trial*

This chapter outlines and discusses a number of models for
understanding the policy process. This includes an outline of what
are described as an *expert* model, a *deliberative* model and a *crisis*
model of the policy process. The conceptions and assumptions
regarding the nature of society and power reflected in each of these
models and the subsequent theories of social action and change are
explored. You may have noticed that for a book on policy analysis,
apart from the introduction, we have not paid much attention,
or at least been explicit, regarding the assumptions being made
about the nature of the problem policy process. The main reason
for this is that part of the purpose of the book is to open up what
is understood about the nature and scope of policy and policy
analysis. Consequently, the first two sections have sought to show
the range of questions that may be asked as part of attempts to
understand the problem policy process. However, now the task is
not only to read and write policy, but also to perform policy. This
involves an engagement with the problem policy process, so the
question of how this is to be understood should not be put off any
longer.

To this end, the oft-cited list in Hogwood and Gunn (1984) identifies
ten different uses of the term policy, which provides a good

illustration of the diversity of the terrain to be covered. The term policy may be used to describe a field of activity (eg social policy), or applied to more specific areas, such as housing policy, through to the decisions of government, and specific programmes of activity and processes. In the interests of attempting to open up the policy field rather than identifying a preferred model, this chapter will highlight a number of models of the policy process (Colebatch, 2006; Hill, 2005; Marsh and Smith, 2001; Sabatier, 1999). These models constitute a typology that does not seek to provide a comprehensive account of all the different theories of the policy process but gives us different ways of thinking about and engaging with policy. Consequently, each model will not only bring different aspects of the problem policy process to the fore, which then become amenable to analysis and action, but will also serve to highlight the different assumptions that underpin them (Dowding, 1995).

In a similar vein to the discussion of the role of the policy analyst in Chapter 4, the models are an attempt to make sense of the literature on the problem policy process as well as an aid in the development of reflexive policy praxis. That is, performing policy is not just about choosing which model to adopt and what form of action to take, but also about considering the assumptions that are being made about the world and the criteria of what counts as a good action and measure of success. This is considered important because, even if policy actors are in a position to agree a 'goal', when it comes to the question of the means to be employed in achieving that goal, a number of options are available and a way of making sense of these options is therefore required.

MODEL MAKING

As discussed in Chapter 6, policy actors use frames when making sense of the problem policy process. That is, policy actors possess bundles of related assumptions that form conceptual lenses for making sense of practice. These frames will provide insight, but they will also distort. That is, while a particular frame will draw attention to particular relations and practices, other features will be neglected (Morgan, 2006). In this respect, it is argued that policy actors have no real choice over whether to use 'theory' or not, the only choice is whether to be implicit or explicit about the assumptions that are reflected and realised in policies and practices (Simpson and Connor, 2011). A consideration of different models can therefore help policy actors develop an awareness of their own practice and the applicability of a particular model for performing policy (Allison, 1971). Following Hogwood and Gunn (1984), these models have a number of functions, namely that they seek to describe both how the problem policy process currently operates and how it should work. In the context of this book, these two functions are considered to go hand in hand, in that the models provide us with a way of looking at the problem policy process, while also posing the question of how should the policy process work.

EXPERT MODEL

Most frequently described as the rational model, the expert model of policy making foregrounds the use of knowledge and expertise in the shaping of decisions. Accounts of the expert model are provided by Bridgman and Davis (2000), Ham and Hill (1984), Hogwood and Gunn (1984), Lasswell (1950, 1951), Simon (1957) and Spicker (2006). Although there are variations (Bridgman and Davis, 2003; Howlett and Ramesh, 2003), normally the expert model outlines a number of steps, phases, stages or sequences, presented in a linear or cyclical pattern, that lead towards a decision regarding the nature of the problem and resulting policies. These are:

○ identifying and examining the social problem;

○ identifying possible options for resolving the problem;

○ assessing the advantages and disadvantages of each option;

○ making a choice about the best option against clear criteria;

○ implementing the policy;

○ assessing and evaluating the outcome (possibly).

Hogwood and Gunn (1984) highlight Simon's (1957) and Lindblom's (1959) models as subtle but significant variations on this broad conception of expert and rational policy making. In Simon's model, values are considered alongside potential options, through a process of intelligence gathering: assessing the pros, cons and consequences of all the options, ordering the options according to the criteria and values of the policy actor and, finally, the policy option chosen. In contrast, Lindblom places the establishment of objectives at the beginning of the process. That is, the policy actor begins by defining and ranking their own 'governing values' and identifying the objectives compatible with these values, before going on to identify all the means and options for achieving these stated objectives, consider and compare the consequences of these particular options and then choose the option(s) that are thought to maximise the values and objectives identified at the start of the model.

However, what these variations share is the distinction that is drawn between problem identification, policy making, policy implementation and policy evaluation. So there is a division of labour where decision making at each stage of the policy-making process is subject to the influence of experts. The nature of the expertise, eg research, technical support, management, topic specific, will depend on the stage of the policy process, but at all stages the expertise is considered to be independent and objective. In this respect, expert policy making tends to operate within and associated with what can be broadly described as a bureaucratic/administrative form.

○ Scientific methods and rigorous, independent and objective evidence are used to determine the 'best' decisions.

○ A distinction is drawn between the formulation, design and organisation of policies and the implementation of these policies. Policy makers think and policy workers implement.

○ Activities are co-ordinated and managed by senior policy actors who possess legal rational authority over the process as a whole.

○ Lines of accountability follow this hierarchy, with guidance being passed down the line of command and communications passing up or down this hierarchy without missing out any steps.

○ The best qualified are identified for particular tasks and then they are trained to perform this pre-designed task.

○ Task and policy performance is monitored. The policy process and its outcomes are assessed against the independent and objective and goals that have been established previously to ensure that procedures are followed and appropriate results achieved.

○ All decisions are made impersonally and neutrally – *sine ira ac studio* – without anger or passion, and normally with reference to an explicitly stated set of rules and provisions.

In this way, for the policy actor seeking to perform within the expert model of policy making, the onus is on identifying credible and evidenced arguments and being able to make this information available and relevant to the appropriate stage of the policy process. For instance, being qualified as an expert involves researching and publishing papers in the relevant academic/industry journal and/ or producing policy briefs. An emphasis may also be placed on gaining access or responding to opportunities to attend formal and official sites of policy making and deliberation, eg select committees, consultation exercises, think-tank seminars, study tours. This may also require learning the official language, rules and procedures for operating in the formal, expert and rational policy spaces.

While what has been described here may be considered to be a caricature, if not a straw man, this has been done in order to highlight that some of the underlying assumptions are remarkably widespread, both in thinking and practice in the problem policy process. This may help explain why the expert model might be considered a self-evident and common-sense way of conceiving policy, as it tends to reflect the way that policy is first introduced to people. Similarly, the institutions that are appointed to enact policies may tend to reflect the distinctions drawn by this expert rational model, as noted above, in their degree of functional specialisation, hierarchy of authority, system of rules and impersonality.

Notably, if operating within this model, even the harshest critics of a particular policy or outcome will tend to attribute blame to the decision making and expertise used to shape policy, rather than the form of 'policy making' and wider social, political and economic relations. That is, it is assumed that expert policy actors will and should deliberate, consider and assess the information and options that are available at each stage of the process. Therefore, if policies are considered to have failed, attention is drawn to the nature of the information that was available or errors in the form or actual decisions that have been made. Put another way, there is still faith in the idea that with the right information and the right system the right policies and outcomes will be produced. Objectivity, rationality and evidence-based policy and practice is considered *both possible and preferable*, and any problems influencing practitioners and policy makers can be solved through the development of better data (Whitelaw and Williams, 1994, p 521).

However, more fundamental criticisms are that the expert model tends to hide rather than address the irrational aspects of the problem policy process. That is, the expertise, technical jargon and the system of rules offer only a veneer of rationality and objectivity. In this respect, policy actors are not simply neutral executors of policy. Even if they do not reflect their personal and political agendas, the system of rules and priorities reflects an ossified ideology and set of interests. In response, proponents of the expert model may argue that they are more than aware of the plurality of interests that have the potential to bias the problem policy process, but by seeking to identify independent and systematic methods and evidence, such difficulties can be transcended. This also provides the basis of a response to critics who suggest that the expert model does not reflect reality. In this regard, the expert model is not so much considered a description of policy making but a normative ideal to be realised. However, this normative ideal can itself be questioned. Apart from questions of whether it is possible to have independent and objective data, the expert model has the potential to become a closed system far removed from the population it serves and, as such, is not only slow to respond to changing environments, but its inherent paternalism exhibits anti-democratic qualities.

DELIBERATIVE MODEL

The deliberative model reflects the notion that a number of diverse policy actors are and should be able to influence, shape and perform

policy. Both reflecting and considered a vital constituent of broader
conceptions of a deliberative society (Dewey, 1927; Elster, 1998;
Habermas, 1996; Rawls, 1993), as a normative ideal, a deliberative
model of the problem policy process requires communication that
leads policy actors to reflect on their position and preferences
in a non-coercive manner (Dryzek, 2000). This refers not just to
the claims-making aspects of the process, but also to the making,
implementation and assessment of policies, at least as defined
by the expert model. In the deliberative model, depending on the
form it takes, in theory, every policy actor should have the right
and potential to influence and perform policy. Consequently,
resources are widely distributed throughout society, as at least
some influence is available to nearly every policy actor. In this way,
no one policy actor dominates. Even in those instances where a
particular policy actor is able to exert considerable influence with
regard to a particular topic or area, this influence is not sustainable
over the problem policy process as a whole, simply due to the
sheer number and diversity of competing positions exhibited by
other policy actors. Admittedly, some of these policy actors may
well be larger, better funded and therefore more influential than
others (Kingdon, 2011), but, once again, the competition provided
by the proliferation of policy actors provides a check and balance
against the predominance of a particular position (Dahl, 1971) and
the power of any one policy actor tends to cancel out the power
of another. The compromises, agreements and trades that can
characterise deliberative approaches may be considered to achieve
consensus, equilibrium, inertia or stalemate, depending on how
positive the outcome is viewed.

In this respect, the deliberative model draws attention to the
messiness and multiplicity of the problem policy process, where
policy actors operate through, around and within the institutional
relations afforded by the expert model (Colebatch, 2005, 2006;
Hajer, 2003; Newman, 2012; Olsson and Hysing, 2012). This is not
to suggest that the deliberative model is 'irrational', but that the
positions of policy actors and the blurring of formal and informal
networks and relations are brought to the fore (Heclo, 1972).

As dramatic changes are unlikely due to the opposition that will be posed by competing groups, policy actors tend to make incremental changes to existing policies and practices. Radically different policies tend not to even be considered as what is considered feasible is likely to be only marginally different from the current consensus. In this way, reforms and relatively minor revisions of existing relations tend to take precedence over any positions that may be considered to rock the boat. If any major change is to take place, it may well occur through a series of small steps over a significant period of time. The problem policy process is thus sometimes characterised as *muddling through* (Lindblom, 1959).

As the problem policy process is populated by a number of relatively small groups, influence can never be assumed within the deliberative model. Particular policy actors will seek the support of others and multiple streams of policy activity may be in evidence (Sabatier, 1993; Sabatier and Jenkins-Smith, 1993). Calls for support may also be exhibited through attempts to create coalitions and networks in order to achieve particular goals and shape the problem policy process (Newman, 2012; Olsson and Hysing, 2012). Policy actor networks may develop as groups of individuals and organisations that share similar belief systems, codes of conduct and established patterns of behaviour may coalesce (Beresford and Holden, 2000; Fawcett and Daugbjerg, 2012; Marsh and Rhodes, 1992). These networks may vary as to their density, diversity or reach. Some networks may offer a relatively open and flexible system of relationships, while policy communities may form as relatively tight-knit groups of experts seek to secure access in particular realms of the problem policy process. For instance, political parties, trades unions, professional and industry associations, corporate lobbyists, institutional interests, third-sector organisations and formal and informal coalitions of like-minded citizens are all considered to influence the problem policy process. Policy actors may initiate campaigns that make use of a number of communication strategies, such as public relations, advertisers, opinion polls and focus groups, in an attempt to gain support from the multitude. This also explains why various forms of mass media may well prove an important site of contestation within a deliberative model (Fischer, 2003).

In those instances where only a few policy actors are willing or able to be involved or particular positions are under-represented, then a small number of policy actors may have an undue influence over the problem policy process. Clearly, proponents of a deliberative model consider this a significant problem. In response, a premium is placed on identifying the 'rules of the game' that enable everyone to have the opportunity to perform policy. For instance, a variant of a deliberative model, admittedly one that privileges the actions of a relatively small number of policy actors, at least when compared to the population as a whole, is provided by Dahl's (1971) characteristics of a polyarchy.

o   Control over government decisions about policy is constitutionally vested in elected officials.

o   Elected officials are chosen and removed in fair and free elections.

o   Practically all adults have the right to vote in these elections.

o   Most adults have the right to become candidates in these elections.

o   Citizens have the right to freedom of expression. This includes the right to criticise officials, the government and the political, economic and social system.

o   Citizens have access to multiple and diverse sources of information alternative sources of information. No government or institutions should monopolise information.

o   Finally, citizens have the right to form and join autonomous associations. This includes political parties and interest groups. These associations can then attempt to influence the government by lobbying, taking part in elections and by other legal and peaceful means.

In this manner, discussion and practices attend as much to the operations of policy making, ensuring multiple viewpoints are accommodated or resolved, as they do to the substantive topics and outcomes. The deliberative model is subject to a number of cautionary notes and criticisms (Dodge, 2010; Dryzek, 2000). This may include questioning whether such a model is desirable or achievable. With respect to the former, it is the public's capacity, expertise and willingness to attend to the demands of the problem policy process that is doubted. With respect to the latter, the debate focuses on what processes and mechanisms need to be put in place to enable a deliberative process to take place.

CRISIS MODEL

A crisis can be described as a sudden shock, interruption or a failure of existing social relations and practices. As such, a crisis is considered to stress and destabilise existing relations and practices. When faced with a crisis, questions are asked as to whether the existing arrangements can sustain the stress, need to be strengthened, or whether new relations and practices need to be put in place in order to deal with and respond to the new circumstances. Therefore crises are associated with periods of uncertainty when people look to identify what is happening and what should be done. A crisis can be felt at a personal, interpersonal, regional, national or global level and may have a number of origins and forms of expression. War, disease, famine, 'natural' disasters, extreme weather and migrations of populations can all present shocks to existing social relations and practices and lead to calls for changes to be made to the provision of social policies. A crisis may have its origin in economic relations, for instance, the oil shocks of 1973 and 1979, the stock market collapse, 'Black Monday' in October 1987 and the subsequent global recession of the early 1990s, and the 'financial' crisis, considered to be triggered by the collapse of the sub-prime mortgage market, in 2007/08 (Starke, Kaasch and van Hooren, 2011). Similarly, increased levels of crime, riots, protests and moral panics may also be cited as crises that require a policy response. Individual events, such as the neglect of individuals or the failure, abuse and corruption of institutions, may also be cast as crises and lead to calls for action to be taken. Finally, new information or knowledge may also lead to a crisis, as people come to question their existing understanding of the world around them.

There are significant differences concerning whether a crisis is the result of an external shock to the system or an inherent characteristic and therefore the inevitable result of existing relations and practices (Marx, 1867/2005). Similarly, social policies may be seen as part of the response to the crisis (Farnsworth and Irving, 2011) or the site, if not the cause, of the crisis (Murray, 1984, 1988). For the purposes of this chapter, it is the struggle over the identification of an event as a crisis and the nature of the response that is considered a vital part of the problem policy process, particularly when policy making is seen from a crisis model perspective.

Hall (1993) and Hay (1999, 2001) have drawn on the work of Kuhn (1962) in an attempt to make sense of such dynamics within the problem policy process. Kuhn argued that scientific progression is best understood in terms of the emergence and establishment of a succession of paradigms. However, periodically, the scientific assumptions that underpin such a paradigm are challenged and overturned, resulting in a paradigmatic 'revolution'. This is described as a period of normal science followed by a period of exceptional science, which then becomes established as a new normal. The vital question being what accounts for this paradigm shift?

During phases of what Kuhn describes as 'normal science', a single paradigm provides the framework for identifying what counts as a legitimate problem, methods, techniques and criteria of 'goodness'. During this period the form of thinking and practice described by the normal science paradigm is predominant, internalised and remains largely unchallenged. However, during this normal period, a number of experiences and experimental outcomes may fail to conform to the predictions of current theories. This may lead some entrepreneurial, outsider or 'maverick' scientists to search for alternative theoretical approaches that might account for (and resolve) the anomalies of the dominant/normal paradigm. An accumulation of exceptions or, for the purposes of this discussion, a shock to the system, may lead scientists to turn to these 'mavericks' and break from the paradigm and the constraints it imposes in order to attend to these anomalies.

Subsequently, in what is described as a period of exceptional science, a new space is opened up, and in time this has the potential to become the new orthodoxy.

Hall (1993) and Hay (1999, 2001) sought to examine the degree to which such a dialectical dynamic was evident in the problem policy process. That is, periods of normal policy making are also relatively ordered and stable – where change tends to be evolutionary rather than revolutionary. The stability of the normal period is in part ensured as policy actors internalise the norms and conventions. In this way, a dominant paradigm sets the parameters for what are considered legitimate and appropriate policy actions. By establishing the frames through which policy actors come to understand the problem policy process, the paradigm serves to set the acceptable limits for what are considered feasible policy relations and practices. As such, the paradigm may not be challenged, at least not by those operating within the normal paradigm.

However, as described above, a set of anomalies or a shock may well lead to a challenge to this normal period of policy making. Those within the normal policy-making paradigm may claim that this shock is not in fact a crisis and does not present a challenge to existing relations and practices; therefore, all that is required is for the normal paradigm to adapt to this aberration. Alternatively, those within the normal paradigm may concede that there is indeed a crisis, but that no feasible alternative is available, therefore it may be a case of reaffirming and bolstering the relations and practices of the normal paradigm. However, if those seeking an alternative are able to establish that this shock is not just an aberration but constitutes a crisis and that a legitimate alternative is available, then a period of exceptional policy making may be realised. Consequently, within this exceptional period, the scope of what is considered politically, socially and economically possible and desirable is reconfigured. Change at this point tends to be relatively rapid and radical (ie from the root) as relations and practices are transformed. The parameters that previously limited policy relations and practices are redrawn and replaced.

Notably, the exceptional period of policy making seeks not just to challenge the content or aims of policies but also to transform the scope of what is seen as policy making and the nature of the institutions, relations and processes involved in the problem policy process. However, it is assumed that there is no determined or uniform policy response to crisis, or even whether a shock comes to be deemed a crisis. To this end, Starke, Kaasch and van Hooren (2011) identify five types of policy response.

○   Non-reaction: no significant changes in existing social arrangements.

○   Incremental expansion: a relatively minor expansion, tension or increase in existing practices or relations, eg more of the same.

○   Incremental retrenchment: a relatively minor restriction, contraction or decrease of existing practice, eg less of the same.

○   Transformative expansion: new policy principles and new programmes, instruments, relations and practices are introduced – normally associated with an increased emphasis on the role of the state in the provision of social policies.

○   Transformative retrenchment: new principles and new programmes, instruments, relations and practices are introduced – normally associated with a restructuring or a reduction in the direct provision of social policies by the state and an increased emphasis on the role of the for-profit (market), third sector (voluntary, independent, not-for-profit) and individuals, families and communities.

When explaining the different responses, consideration needs to be given to the existing arrangements, both in terms of size and scale, principles, institutions, relations and practices. For example, Nation A may undergo transformative expansion and Nation B transformative retrenchment, but this may result in a convergence of policy regimes if Nation A is seen as starting from a position where it has a 'smaller' state, with lower levels of public provision and more individualistic values than Nation B, whose starting position is a 'bigger state', with a relatively higher level of public provision and more collective values. Similarly, the relative strength of the different social, political and economic interests may have an impact on the degree to which events are considered to be a crisis and the nature of the response.

Paradigm shifts are relatively rare and tend to be associated with the spectacular politics of crisis and contestation. It should also be noted that paradigm shifts are rarely merely a reflection of a change of mind or viewpoint but involve a reordering of material interests. That is, those policy actors who benefit from the relations and practices of the existing regime may well resist any attempt to overturn the order. Conversely, those outside the dominant paradigm are by definition marginalised by the existing relations and may either seek to enter the dominant paradigm or to transform the existing order. The crux of the argument, then, is that the problem policy process is a site of struggle between antagonistic relations. In this respect, in the crisis model, although the state is an important site for analysis and action, it is not necessarily taken as the beginning or end of political action. Consequently, the actions of the policy actor will in part depend on their position within the dominant paradigm. If they are operating within the consensus and happy to continue operating with this, then it will be about operating according to the values, relations and practices made available through the dominant paradigm and resisting any transformation of these relations. However, for those policy actors who are operating outside of the dominant paradigm, in the 'wilderness' years, efforts may be placed on establishing a legitimate and credible alternative and then when the existing relations do experience a shock, persuading people that this event is to be seen as a crisis and taking the opportunity to ensure that the alternative is adopted and 'mainstreamed'. A corollary of this position is that those who are not willing, permitted or able to operate within the dominant paradigm may well need to create alternative spaces in which to perform policy. Therefore, the crisis model draws attention to the role of campaigns, protests and forms of direct action that have helped shape the problem policy process in the past and continue to provide a legitimate means of operating in the future. In this regard, it is asserted that there is no social policy without a coalition of interests of a social movement capable of imposing it (Bourdieu and Wacquant, 2001, p 56).

PICKING UP THE THREADS

This chapter is not considered to be definitive or comprehensive, but it offers a way into making sense of and engaging with the wide range of approaches and practices regarding the problem policy process. The reader is strongly encouraged to follow some of the threads that have been picked at in this chapter. However, as you follow a particular line of inquiry, and become immersed in the questions, methods and debates of a particular model and tradition for understanding the problem policy process, you are also asked to come back to this chapter and take a view across the different models and what all these perspectives can offer for your practice.

Put another way, if a particular way of seeing becomes frustrating, both in terms of the process and outcomes, you may be well served to consider alternative routes. It should be borne in mind, however, that although there are questions of incommensurability across these different models so that attempting to create a supra-model is not necessarily recommended, each model does offer a different entry point into understanding and engaging in the problem policy process. However, as stated previously, this is not to suggest that it is just a question of rethinking the world but rather of considering your position in relation to the world. When performing policy, it is necessary to consider the capacity of a policy actor, or what has been described in this book as the policy actor's potential. For example, the expert model will privilege qualifications, the capacity to undertake research, knowledge of the relevant systems and practices and access to the principal decisions makers. Alternatively, the deliberative model will foreground knowledge and skills that enable the policy actor to network, communicate, frame issues, mobilise support, set agendas, negotiate and engage in forms of practical argumentation (Fairclough and Fairclough, 2012). Finally, depending on the policy actor's position in relation to the dominant paradigm, it will be their ability to manufacture consent or create and take advantage of events and dissent that may prove pivotal. Consequently, each model has different criteria for assessing the capacity of a policy actor to engage in the problem policy process.

8   Power

The Eagle and the Arrow

An Eagle was soaring through the air when suddenly it heard the whizz of an Arrow, and felt itself wounded. Slowly it fluttered down to the earth, with its life-blood pouring out of it. Looking down upon the Arrow with which it had been pierced, it found that the shaft of the Arrow had been feathered with one of its own plumes. "Alas!" it cried, as it died.

Aesop

This chapter discusses the importance and role of power in efforts to perform policy. A brief outline of some of the different notions of power is provided. Similar to elsewhere in the book, the aim is not to posit one approach over another, but to illustrate how each approach brings different aspects to the fore, while also neglecting others. Each approach to power also makes different assumptions about how the policy actor should then engage with the form of power being described. It is this question of how to engage with power that is considered most vital in attempts to perform policy.

When making an observation such as *she has got a lot of power*, power is being referred to as if it is an object – that is something that can be mined, owned, exchanged, used and, therefore, diminish with use. It follows, then, that power is something you have either got or have not got and this raises the question of what this power looks like, what it consists of and where it can be obtained. Such an image of power is understandable as it may appear to correspond with people's experience of the exercise of power: people with power use it to control, shape and influence others who possess little or no power. However, alongside this object view of power, in this chapter, power is also discussed in more relational terms. This is where power is not considered to be an object that can exist outside of the actors who exercise it (Dowding, 1996; Piven, 2008). Rather, power exists in and through the relations that hold between different actors and in this respect it is closer to the Latin root of the term power, *potere*, meaning 'to be able' (Isaac, 1987, p 21). From this perspective, power broadly refers to the capacity to affect things. The rest of this chapter examines the different dimensions of power that have been conceived and their implications for attempts to perform policy.

FIRST DIMENSION OF POWER – GETTING SOMEONE TO DO WHAT THEY OTHERWISE WOULD NOT DO

This first dimension understands power as a causal relation between two parties (Simon, 1953). In this respect, power is equivalent to the force that is necessary to change the behaviour of another individual (Dahl, 1957). One of the advantages of viewing power in this way is that it becomes something to be observed and studied. That is, how does Person A (cause) get Person B to do something they otherwise wouldn't do (effect) (Dahl, 1957)?

Studies of power, then, focus on identifying specific exercises of such power and observable conflict (Polsby, 1980). To this end, attention is paid to identifying what Person B would have done in the absence of Person A. This may be achieved by identifying Person B's preferences and then seeing if there is a difference between what they want to do and their actual behaviour. So, if it is possible to identify that Person B is doing something that they would not want to do if it were not for Person A, then it is possible to claim that an instance of power has been identified. For the first dimension of power the powerful are revealed by their capacity to exercise power over the powerless – defined as those who are unable to pursue their preferences as a result of the actions of the powerful.

This first dimension of power may be most immediate when considering conflict in interpersonal relationships, where the use of direct physical force and restraint are in evidence, eg physical assault. However, it is also a concept of power that can inform an understanding of the problem policy process. That is, by examining the various policy actors' preferences and the decisions that are made and whose preferences have been met, it is then possible to begin to develop hypotheses about those actors with power and those without. We can then continue to test these hypotheses by continuing to identify preferences, the decisions that are made and the relationship between these outcomes and the actors' preferences. Vital questions to be asked as part of this first dimension of power are:

○ what are the various positions and relations and who dominates?

○ what resources are needed and what is the distribution of these resources?

○ who has access to these resources and how are they allocated?

○ how are decisions made and by whom?

○ what are the relations between the various actors?

○ what are the lines of accountability?

○ who prescribes the activity of others?

○ what are the sanctions and rewards for various actors?

○ who are the policy actors responsible for monitoring the activities of others, establishing the criteria for what counts as good and enforcing the sanctions and rewards?

This is a particularly useful approach if analysis is to move beyond broad ascriptions of *powerful elites and forces* to a point where we are then able to identify the exercise of this power (Dahl, 1958). Clearly for those in the problem policy process, this is not just an academic exercise but may be the basis of challenging these instances of power. However, this dimension of power has been subject to criticism, and it is one of the alternatives to such a conception that is now discussed.

SECOND DIMENSION OF POWER – SETTING THE AGENDA

This second dimension of power brings the notion of non-decision to the fore when attempting to understand power (Bachrach and

Baratz, 1962; Kingdon, 2011). A non-decision refers to the thwarting
or suppression of a potential or actual challenge to the position of
the decision maker. This second dimension of power was developed
partly in response to two notable criticisms of the first dimension of
power (Bachrach and Baratz, 1962). Namely that:

○ conceptions of power cannot be considered limited to those
  instances where power can be observed;

○ conceptions of power can also be found in instances where
  conflict has been suppressed.

The second dimension of power therefore sought to extend the
scope of what is taken to be power. This includes a move beyond
observable episodes of conflict between different parties to those
instances where power has resulted in the limitation of interaction.
For example, although the absence of conflict would appear to open
up the concept of power to a point where power is everywhere,
the decisions and actions that create this non-event do need to be
considered and are traceable. For example, networks of close-knit
policy actors may be resistant to new entrants. In this respect,
attention extends beyond instances of decision making and includes
the identification of the values, beliefs, practices, rituals and
procedures that are seen to operate for the benefit of some and at
the expense of others.

A rather mundane, but no less significant operation of this second
dimension can be understood with regard to the setting of the
agenda. In its most literal sense, this means what items are to be
discussed at a meeting. If the item is not even included on the
agenda, there is no opportunity for the discussion to take place
(non-event and thwarted conflict), never mind for a challenge to
be levelled. In a more figurative sense of the term, where agenda is
taken to mean the predominance of particular social and political
values and institutional practices, if a particular social policy or
policy option is not part of the agenda, once again, any potential
conflict or challenge that might result from such a discussion has
been avoided.

In this way, the second dimension of power seeks to capture and reflect the institutional rules and operation of the 'game' that lead to a mobilisation of bias (Schattschneider, 1960) operating for the powerful and against the powerless. This is an exercise that involves both observation and the use of judgements as to the significance and degree of bias and power being exercised. Important questions to be asked include:

- who sets the agenda and defines the problem (Kingdon, 2011)?

- are all parties able to make a contribution or is the setting of the agenda the preserve of particular policy actors?

- what, or more specifically, whose language and imagery is used in the communication of the problem policy process?

- what values and positions are reflected in this language and imagery?

- what sites and spaces are used?

- who decides which sites and spaces are used and the arrangements of relations in the problem policy process?

This second dimension of power, particularly when combined with the insights provided by the first dimension of power, can help explain why policies appear to exhibit inertia – where particular ideas and practices stick. That is, not only are the opportunities to speak truth to power limited, but even when opportunities are made available, there would appear to be little benefit to be gained from deputations and the presentation of evidence and reason. So how can this power be resisted and challenged? Essentially, this would include efforts to shape and change the agenda by applying pressure to the policy actors who currently set the agenda, for example, through public campaigns, protests or lobbying. Alternatively, this type of power may be challenged by seeking to reconfigure the relations and practices of those involved in setting the agenda. This refers to those activities that seek to increase participation and open up new forms of representation into the problem policy process, or even creating alternative spaces for deliberation and actions outside of the existing relations for setting the agenda.

THIRD DIMENSION OF POWER – SHAPING PREFERENCES

If the first two dimensions of power reflect the capacity of policy actors to pursue or exhibit their preferences, then the third dimension attends to the role of power to shape people's preferences. It is one thing to get someone to act against their will, and another to shape the agenda, but imagine the power of being able to shape preferences and therefore secure willing compliance (Lukes, 1974). The extended logic of such a position is that if the preferences of the dominated could be shaped to match the preferences of those who seek to dominate, the first two dimensions become redundant as the powerless now want what the powerful want. No further coercion or mobilisation of bias is required.

What is notable about this third dimension of power is that, beyond asserting its presence, how is this operation of power to be identified? In the first and second dimensions of power, where actors were denied the opportunity to pursue or consider their preferences, the mismatch between different actors' preferences and their realisation offered a point of entry into understanding instances of power. With the third dimension, this is no longer possible. Namely, if an actor's preferences are identified as matching the preferences of those deemed powerful, how is it possible to distinguish between an actual agreement and an instance of Lukes' third dimension of power. The response to such a situation is to posit the notion of *objective interests* (Dowding, 2006; Lukes, 1974). Putting aside the contentious question of how such objective interests would be identified, for the purpose of this discussion, if it is assumed that an observer is able to identify what an actor's interests are better than the actor themselves then this solves the conundrum raised above. Namely, if an actor's stated preferences and actions deviate from what has been identified as their objective interests, then it is possible for the policy analyst to state that not only is the actor exhibiting a *false consciousness* (Lukacs, 1920/1971), but also a third dimension of power may be in operation. As noted above, further support for such a hypothesis is provided when the actor's preferences match those deemed powerful and dominating, and therefore the actors are seen as operating against, or at least resigned to the impossibility of, achieving their true interests (Scott, 1990).

What is also of interest in this third dimension of power is that this manipulation of interests and preferences does not need to be the result of a specific and discrete intervention by one actor over another (Isaac, 1987; Lukes, 1974). Rather, in part an extension of the second dimension of power, it refers to the structuring of relations and practices that inculcate a dominant, hegemonic (Gramsci, 2003) set of values. In this respect, the power that is exercised does not even need to be intentional. The dominators, those whose objective interests are met by the prevailing order, are not necessarily the architects of this exercise of power, but do benefit from it and therefore will seek to continue and conserve such relations. Similarly, some accounts of Foucault's notions of power relations and fields of knowledge, expressed through the term discourses, suggests a total but hidden form of social control (Hartsock, 1990). In sum, the third dimension of power draws attention to the structuring of relations in addition to the actions of specific actors.

With respect to efforts to perform policy, the scope for action may appear rather limited. First, there is a question of how any actors are to escape this totality. That is, if the structured relationship embodies the dominators' and exploiters' values and practices, how is this all-embracing grasp to be escaped (Piven, 2008)? Assuming escape from this manufactured consent is possible, given the benefits accrued by those who dominate and exploit through existing relations, there would appear to be little to be gained in seeking to make a case to those in power. Rather, for those who are able to escape this manufactured consent (Herman and Chomsky, 1998), first and foremost, efforts may go into breaking people's false consciousness and seeking to highlight their true interests (Gramsci, 2003). This may involve efforts to reveal the operation of the existing social and political relations, for instance, by picking at the veneer of rationality and pointing out the inconsistencies and contradictions of existing relations (Shore and Wright, 1997). By revealing the interests masked by a supposed rationality, claims that the problem policy process reflects a natural, objective, rational and impartial account are destabilised.

Second, efforts would then go into securing social relations that do reflect and realise people's true interests. Clearly this would appear to establish an antagonistic relationship with those who to date have sought to dominate and exploit the 'people'. Hence, this involves an attempt to move from an alleged consensus to the creation or, more accurately, a revealing, of the conflict and antagonism that structures social, political and economic relations. Subsequently, the aim would be to realise a transformation of social, political and economic relations. Apart from questions of how such an 'escape' is possible, the desirability or otherwise of a vanguard leading such a transformation, or what should take the place of existing relations, there is also the question as to where the possible points for intervention are when power appears to be exercised through the structures and system as a whole.

FOURTH DIMENSION OF POWER – DISRUPTIVE POWER

Despite the clear differences between these three dimensions of power, there does appear to be one clear point of comparison – the notion that power is held over people (Isaac, 1987). That is, the emphasis is on the power of Person A to exercise power over Person B, contrary to Person B's preferences and interests. The source of this power may be varied, eg violence, economic or cultural resources, but it is broadly understood as a resource that Person A has access to that Person B does not, or at least as an asymmetry of access to this resource. Such exercises of power are not to be denied, but it would appear to leave little room for anything but a self-perpetuating set of hierarchical relations (Piven, 2008). This is because resources exploitable for exercising power will accumulate at the top of the hierarchy, thus reinforcing and sustaining the power of those already in positions of privilege. The logic of these first three dimensions of power is therefore that those deemed to be at the dominated or exploited end of the relationships, by definition, have very little power to resist, never mind challenge and overturn these relations. Such accounts are useful for examining how power relations are sustained and in highlighting that there are 'victims' of dominant and exploitative relationships, but they may also deny these 'victims' agency and capacity to act. And yet, there are instances when people who are deemed to be powerless do exercise power, not only revealing their agency, but also interrupting and on occasion reconfiguring, if not transforming, social, political and economic relations (Piven, 2008). In an attempt to explain the exercise of power by the powerless, a number of writers have sought to provide an interdependent account of power (Arendt, 1970; de Beauvoir, 1949/2010; Elias, 1969; Fanon, 1961/2004; Firestone, 1970/2003; Foucault, 1980; Gandhi, 1962; Isaac, 1987; Marx, 1867/2005; Piven, 2008). Each of these writers develops their accounts in different ways, particularly with regard to the significance of particular relationships and the actions to be taken, but for the purposes of this discussion, it is argued that they all attend to the disruptive potential offered by these interdependent relationships.

As noted, the starting point for attending to this fourth dimension of power is the interdependent and complex network of relations and practices that constitute the problem policy process. The question is not who possesses power, but how such power is exercised and its consequences (Foucault, 1980). Take a moment to consider all the relations and practices necessary to complete the most everyday tasks, the transportation of goods and people, the infrastructure and work required to ensure an energy supply, the operations that secure the networks of communication that have become a given, the frequently hidden labour and relations that go into the caretaking and maintenance of individuals, families, institutions, public spaces and the extended and far-reaching supply chains that are now involved in the production of the most mundane goods. Now think for a moment what happens if just one of the links in this chain of interdependence 'breaks'. Whether this break is intended or not, the net result is that the ebb and flow of everyday life is disrupted. It is only on these occasions that attention is paid to these particular links in the chain. Consequently, it is these networks of interdependence that not only bring people together and prove to be essential to the existing social order, but also provide numerous sites and opportunities for this acquiescence and co-operation to end, thereby disrupting everyday practices and relations (Piven, 2008). In this fourth-dimension account, then, power does not operate above or beyond people's heads, but is realised and reflected through the fabric of everyday practices and relations (The Free Association, 2011).

In this fourth dimension, all actors are considered to have the potential to disrupt. For example, this disruption may operate on a global, national, institutional or interpersonal level, where states or corporations withdraw funding or capital, services are curtailed or access to resources and benefits is denied. It is this capacity to disrupt that gives the supposed powerless, power (Della Porta and Tarrow, 2005; Doherty, Plows and Wall, 2003; Piven, 2008; Tilley, 2005). For instance, employees rely on employers for employment, but employers also require employees. Similarly, those engaged in paid productive labour depend on those who provide the informal care that ensures the reproduction of this labour, educational institutions require students, retailers require customers and governments depend on the co-operation, if not the approval or direct support, of their 'public' (Piven, 2008). Consequently, when these individuals or groups boycott, occupy, strike, exit, jam, blockade or fail to co-operate, there is the potential not just to disrupt local patterns, but for this disruption to ripple out through the configurations of relations and practices that constitute the problem policy process. Drawing on the work of Reinsborough and Canning (2010), a range of points of intervention can be identified. These points of intervention represent sites and relations where action can be taken to disrupt the problem policy process.

○   Point of production – where products and services are produced and organised (eg strikes, pickets, work to rule, takeovers).

○   Point of destruction – where resources are extracted, pollution is dumped (in an environmental context) or the negative consequences of policies and actions are manifested (eg bearing witness and documenting conditions through journalism or research).

o   Point of consumption – where products and services are purchased (eg boycotts, sit-ins, point-of-purchase demonstrations, 'brand-busting', advocacy).

o   Point of decision – where the authorities and power holders who are responsible and accountable for services and products are located and if appropriate can meet a campaign's demands (eg protests, lobbying, petitions, letter writing, naming and shaming).

o   Points of circulation – actions that interrupt and disrupt the rhythm of life. In its most literal sense those actions that block the circulation of goods and services at an interpersonal level or in wider social, political and economic relations (blockades; non-cooperation; withdrawal of support).

o   Point of assumption – challenging dominant and powerful underlying assumptions. Making alternative narratives available and reframing the debate (eg media monitoring, alternative and independent media, 'subvertisements', 'culture jamming', campaigns).

All of these points of intervention represent potential material practices and sites of action that seek to disrupt and, where necessary, reconfigure those institutions, policies and practices. The point of assumption is less tangible and reflects attempts to challenge and offer alternatives to the myths and assumptions that sustain the status quo (Simpson and Connor, 2011). It is argued that actions at the points of production, destruction, consumption, circulation and destruction are most successful and sustainable when integrated with action at point of assumption.

Disruptive practices may be used at these points of intervention to resist cuts or when making demands for services and benefits. However, a fourth dimension of power may also reflect and realise a constituent power (Hardt and Negri, 2000). This is where the aims are to not only challenge existing social, political and economic relations, but also prefigure alternatives. In this regard, the practices associated a fourth dimension of power may not just be a means to an end, but an end in itself – a move from the *politics of demand* to the *politics of the act* (Day, 2004).

THE PURSUIT OF POWER

What this chapter has sought to achieve is to provide an outline of different dimensions of power. It is clear, even from these brief outlines, that a range of approaches are available and that each one of these dimensions offers not only a different way of understanding power, but affords different sites and scope for action. Depending on the position of the policy actor, each of these dimensions of power may offer potential points of departure for performing policy. However, an important question is whether power can be considered outside of the context in which it is used. Put another way, is an idea of power identified in advance of acting, or does the model of power derive from experience? The position taken in this book is that it is a bit of both. That is, a particular dimension of power may lead us as policy actors to attend to particular features and relations in the problem policy process that then help guide our actions; however, our practice experience, particularly in new contexts, may well then require us to draw on different dimensions, which then bring our attention to new features and potentially new practices, and so on and so on. Put another way, a policy actor may find themselves in a position where the structures appear overwhelming and the opportunity for individual action seems limited. In this context, a model that helps the actor attend to the structures may help them reveal the texture of these structures and see that they are not quite as monolithic or fixed as imagined. Contradictions, inconsistencies and the unsustainable and untenable positions occupied within these structural relations may provide sites for leverage.

Conversely, the models also may provide a source of reflexivity when examining policy practices and the power that we all hold. That is, as part of everyday practice what resources are or are not made available to others through the choices and actions that are taken? Efforts to perform policy demand a sensibility and disposition that not only develops strategies but also is willing to recognise the importance of events and other windows of opportunity in order to advance their position. Used in conjunction with models of the policy process, an engagement with the power that exists through and within the problem policy process can help reveal room for manoeuvre. This means attending to the exercise of power, recognising the shifting positions of policy actors, making judgements as to which actors, institutions, sites and practices are significant and tracing relations between them and, where necessary, not just building networks, but potentially interrupting, changing and recognising networks of practice. In sum, the problem policy process is not just seen as a set of operational manuals and procedures that then govern and define practices. The problem policy process has and arguably requires multiple spaces and opportunities for interpretation, adaptation and negotiation in order to ensure its success.

Recognition of the power that people already possess, never mind the argument that power needs to become an explicit part of people's practice, can lead to a certain degree of unease. It is one thing to understand the nature of power, but quite another to urge people to recognise and, if necessary, develop their own use of power. However, if, as a policy actor, the goal is to perform policy, then it is argued that it will also be necessary to engage and make use of power. What this chapter has sought to highlight is that every policy actor possesses a potential to act. These exercises of power may have different levels of impact and may not always be recognised, at least within more traditional renderings, as exercises of power, but the potential is there. It really is then just a question of if and how that potential is to be developed and the manner in which this power is then exercised. Any unease regarding power is just as likely to stem from the responsibility that comes with realising the power that people already possess as it does from witnessing an overwhelming exercise of power. Intended or not, our actions have power and influence. In this regard, it is not a question of whether you should exercise power, but of how your power has been exercised to date and how it will be exercised in the future.

9   Activities

If we are wrong, not everything will have been lost, because our organising will have produced a populace that questions, that demands, that moves

Baptist and Bricker-Jones (2001)

This chapter highlights three accounts of actions that have been taken by a range of policy actors in an attempt to influence and shape the problem policy process. These accounts include 'Feeble-minded policies', 'The control of tobacco' and the 'Piqueteros'. What is notable is that each of these accounts draws attention to the diversity and range of policy actors, positions, practices, relations and sites of action that constitute the problem policy process. Furthermore, each account appears to draw on different assumptions as to what the nature of the problem is, the justification for acting, what is considered to be an ethical act, the nature of policy making and how power and influence can and should be exercised to achieve given ends. Not only does each account provide a different case study for understanding how policy can be read, written and performed, but it also facilitates an examination of the different policy actor positions and if and how their practices seek to reflect and realise such a position.

FEEBLE-MINDED POLICIES

In Britain, at the same time that a number of landmark pieces of legislation and social reform were being passed and enacted by the Liberal Government of 1906–11, most notably free school meals (1906), school medical inspections (1907), the Children Act (1908), Old Age Pensions (1908), the Labour Exchanges Act (1909) the Housing and Town Planning Act (1909), the Finance Act of 1910 and the introduction of unemployment and health insurance in 1911, a number of politicians, experts and voluntary associations were preoccupied with the problem of the 'feeble-minded'. Drawing principally on the work of Stedman-Jones (1984), Simmons (1978), and Welshman (2006), this account explores the fabrication of the problem of the 'feeble-minded' and the methods used to establish the policies.

Sir Charles Trevelyan, in his capacity as a member of the Council of the Charity Organisation Society, provided what is considered to be the first recorded use of the term 'feeble-minded' in the context of social reform (Simmons, 1978). This term, in the UK at least, was intended to draw a distinction between *irredeemable idiots* and *imbeciles* and those identified as *improvable idiots*, that is, those capable of responding to institutional care and treatment (Simmons, 1978).

A campaign to address the problem of feeble-mindedness and mental deficiency, calling for changes in policy and practice to be enacted, grew out of an increasing concern over the distinctions and relationship between notions of lunacy and normality and the health and vitality of the population as a whole. The introduction of a national elementary school system as a result of the Education Act of 1870 had brought to the attention of the authorities the number of children with a range of physical and mental difficulties (Simmons, 1978). This led to concerns that these children were not well served by the existing schools and that alternative provision needed to be made. Alongside these developments in education from the 1880s onwards, there were also enduring and growing concerns at the state and conditions of the 'poor'. The proposed policy and practices that sought to address the problem of the feeble-minded need to be considered within the context of a wider anxiety concerning the problem of the *social residuum* (Stedman-Jones, 1984).

In 1883 an anonymous penny pamphlet drew attention to the *grim facts* of the urban poor of London. Titled *The Bitter Cry of Outcast London: an Enquiry into the Condition of the Abject Poor*, it created a sensation and helped make the slums of London and beyond the topic of the day (Wohl, 1968). (Authorship has since been attributed at least in part to Andrew Mearns, Secretary of the

London Congregational Union.) The social and political upheaval of the late nineteenth century and the growth of an urban middle class during this period, served to bring into sharp relief an increasing, proximate and stratified population of the 'poor' (Stedman-Jones, 1984; Welshman, 2006). Although differences exist as to the degree to which the residuum was a concern peculiar to the late nineteenth century (Harris, 1995; Hennock, 1976), there is less dispute that the residuum was increasingly subject to investigations and plans for reform during this period. A number of writers sought to locate the origins of the problem of the poor and to then propose the actions to be taken. Most notable among these were the founder of the Salvation Army, William Booth's (1890) *In Darkest England and the Way Out*; Arnold White's (1901/1973) *Efficiency and Empire* and *The Strength of the People* (1902) by Helen Bosanquet, an influential figure in the Charitable Organisation Society. It is notable that the imagery, if not the methods, of the accounts of the exploration and exploits of empire came to inform some of these social commentaries of Britain's own interior (Keating, 1976). An equivalence was drawn between the primitive, uncivilised, exotic, feral and threatening outposts of Britain's empire, such as Stanley's 'Dark Continent' of Africa, and the new problems posed by the 'race apart' in Booth's *Darkest England*. Welshman (2006) notes that a *social residuum* was, directly or indirectly, increasingly a cause for concern in a range of governmental papers – the Royal Commission on the Housing of the Working Classes (1885), the Royal Commission on Labour (1891–94), the select committees on the Distress from Want of Employment (1894–96), the Interdepartmental Committee on Physical Deterioration (1904) and the Royal Commission on the Poor Laws (1905–09).

Arguments were made that at the bottom of this *pauper class* were a particularly physically and morally degenerate and repugnant populace that threatened to overwhelm the *strong* (Stedman-Jones, 1984). Overall, anxiety was expressed that, unless action was taken, this social residuum would infect and weaken the respectable lower orders, if not the social body as a whole. Alarm at the threat posed by the persistent poor was far from new, and throughout the nineteenth century the operation of the Poor Law (1834) and emergence of associations such as the Charitable Organisation Society had sought to discipline, manage and reform this problem group. Towards the end of the nineteenth century, though, concerns over degenerate groups were given credence by the 'new' methods of social investigation and the fledgling 'science' of eugenics (MacNicol, 1983).

The surveys of Charles Booth and Benjamin Seebohm Rowntree are particularly renowned examples of the increasing influence and status given to social investigation as part of attempts to address social problems. However, Margaret Loane's (1910) *Neighbours and Friends* and Dame Florence Bell's (1907) *At the Works* provided and foreshadowed ethnographic accounts of the poor's lives, relations, practices and conditions. For good reason, the work of such investigators can be seen as well-intended and laudable attempts to bring evidence and rationality to the understanding of social problems and the execution of social policies, However, these investigations and subsequent proposals for reform also reflected, and in some instances helped realise, sets of assumptions for understanding society and its problems.

Problems including crime, alcoholism, prostitution and poverty had long been seen as the result of moral or character failings, and the stringent measures enacted by the 1834 Poor Law sought to at best cure or at least discipline such moral failings. Methods of social investigation and their focus on the behaviour and conditions of individuals and communities, rather than the social, political and economic conditions that produced such conditions, offered the potential to survey, identify, categorise and document the relevant problem groups. The 'science' of eugenics was able to locate the failings of these groups within the biology of the individuals who constituted the residuum. The persistence of social problems could now be explained through biology and hereditary factors in particular. Such a position drew on interpretations of Darwin's *Origin of the Species* applied to social and economic theories, for example, Herbert Spencer's use of the term *survival of the fittest* in his *Principles of Biology* (1864). An exemplar of such a viewpoint was provided by White, who, in reference to what he described as the *nomad poor*, noted that: *to enable them by unwise compassion to propagate their kind, is to hand on to posterity a legacy of unmixed evil* (White, 1885, p 716).

The solution, according to eugenics experts, was simple – the feeble-minded were to be separated from the population as a whole and stopped from *reproducing their kind* (Simmons, 1978). As such, the segregation of the feeble-minded was just one of several illiberal practices that were proposed during this period, including the use of labour colonies and plans for the sterilisation of problem groups. It also partly explains why it was the fertility of women, particularly those unmarried and in receipt of poor relief, that was to be the subject of many of the debates, policies and practices in this period (Simmons, 1978). Notably, this was a position that was legitimated by practices and expertise of social investigators, reformers and eugenicists.

So the campaign to care for the feeble-minded represented a combination of very practical concerns about how the 'mentally deficient' should be treated, developments in the surveying and categorisation of problem groups, and an increasingly vocal and influential eugenic argument that the feeble-minded were evidence of a population that posed a threat to the health and vitality of the British race (Harris, 2004; Jones, 1986; Simmons, 1978; Stedman-Jones, 1984; Thomson, 1998). Questions of idiocy and lunacy had been subject to legislation and policy previously, but feeble-mindedness had been perceived as a private problem and therefore was the preserve of families, charitable bodies or the Poor Law Guardians. However, the private troubles of the feeble-minded increasingly came to be seen as a problem not just for individuals and their families but society as a whole.

A Royal Commission on the Care and Control of the Feeble-Minded was established in 1904, eventually reporting in 1908. The scope of the inquiry headed by the Commission was to review the existing methods of dealing with *imbecile, feeble-minded or defective persons*, defining various grades of mental deficiency and developing proposals for the care of *lunatics and mental defectives*.

The Commission also sought to identify any *mental defectives* who were not subject to an institution but were known by the relevant authorities. Doctors A.F. Tregold and W.A. Potts were appointed by the Royal Commission to act as its two chief medical investigators. In order to identify the numbers and grades of mental defectives, 'inebriate' homes, 'lunatic' asylums, prisons, schools and workhouses in sixteen rural and urban districts were visited in England and Wales (Simmons, 1978). The Royal Commission estimated that, excluding certified lunatics, there were 149,628 mental defectives in England and Wales, representing 0.46 per cent of the population as a whole. It was estimated that 44.45 per cent of this population of mental defectives were unquestionably in need of provision either in their own interest or for public safety (Royal Commission for the Care and Control of the Feeble-Minded, 1908).

The final figures can be treated with some scepticism. First, inspectors reported problems when attempting to categorise the 'feeble-minded' and distinguishing between 'social failures' and 'mental defectives'. Second, the figures collected from the typical district were then extrapolated to England and Wales as a whole. However, this did not prevent these findings being used to form the basis of the Commission's recommendations and also being cited in debates on the nature of the legislation to be adopted (Simmons, 1978).

In making their recommendations, a number of principles were established, most notably that those deemed as of *unsound mind*, *lunatics*, *idiots*, *imbeciles*, *feeble-minded*, and as such *mentally defective*, should be given protection by the state (Royal Commission for the Care and Control of the Feeble-Minded, 1908). Furthermore:

○ the mental condition of these persons, and neither their poverty nor their crime is the real ground of their claim for help from the state;

○ the protection of the mentally defective person should be continued for as long as is necessary for his good.

In order to implement these principles, having considered the existing provision, it was recommended that a single central authority be appointed to supervise the local administrative bodies. The board would be constituted by qualified medical men and barristers at law who would be aided by eight assistant commissioners, each of whom should be appointed to supervise a district. A statutory committee would be in place in each local authority and this committee would take over duties for the care of the feeble-minded.

Both during the work of the Commission and following the publication of its report, *The Times* newspaper, the Eugenics Education Society and the National Association for the Care of the Feeble-Minded campaigned strongly for the Commission's recommendations to be enshrined in legislation (Simmons, 1978). For *The Times*, *social failures* were no longer explained solely through lack of character, to be remedied through education and discipline, but there was now also a scientific explanation, mental deficiency, to be considered. The Eugenics Education Society and the National Association for the Care of the Feeble-Minded had formed a joint committee to push for legislation. In 1910, the Committee sent letters to all those candidates standing in the General Election. The letter asked, *Would you undertake to support measures that tend to discourage parenthood on the part of the feeble-minded and other degenerate types?*

In the absence of any initial action being taken by the government, two private members bills were submitted, but in 1912 the government introduced its own bill. During the course of the bill being debated, both the Eugenics Education Society and the National Association for the Care of the Feeble-Minded pressed their case by making presentations at the highest levels of government, This included meetings between the Eugenics Education Society and the Home Secretary, while the National Association for the Care of the Feeble-Minded made their case to the Prime Minister, Lord Chancellor, Home Secretary and President of the Local Government Board. Following several amendments and faced with a small, but stubborn and vocal opposition, the Mental Deficiencies Act of 1913 was eventually passed by a vote of 180 to 3. The Act went into effect on 1 April 1914.

The final Act did not reflect all the recommendations of the Royal Commission's report, but most notably the compulsory institutionalisation of mental defectives was enshrined in law (Simmons, 1978). The Act defined four categories of mental defective – idiots, imbeciles, feeble-minded and moral imbecile. The feeble-minded were defined as *persons in whose case there exists from birth or from an early age mental defectiveness not amounting to imbecility, yet so pronounced that they require care, supervision and control for their own protection or for the protection of others*.

Notably, the compulsory detainment of mentally defective individuals covered by the Act reflected the sites and methods of the Commission. Those who could be institutionalised by the state included those 'defectives' who came to the attention of the authorities because they were already in prisons, lunatic asylums, workhouses, reformatories, or were picked up in the street without visible means of support, habitual drunkards, and those in receipt of poor relief at the time of giving birth to an illegitimate child or when pregnant with such a child (Harris, 2004, p 164–65).

THE CONTROL OF TOBACCO

The World Health Organization (WHO) (2011) estimates that during the twentieth century, tobacco use has caused 100 million deaths. WHO also estimates that if current trends continue, tobacco-related deaths will increase to more than eight million per year by 2030 and, if unchecked, it is forecast that tobacco may cause about one billion deaths in the twenty-first century. In response, the WHO is a particularly vivid example of how a number of public health and health promotion organisations have sought to fight what is described as a global tobacco epidemic. In 2003 the WHO Framework Convention on Tobacco Control was adopted by the

World Health Assembly and entered into force in 2005. Considered to represent a milestone in tobacco control, the convention reaffirms the right of people to the highest standard of health, provides legal dimensions for international health co-operation and sets high standards for compliance (WHO, 2003). In an effort to provide tangible practices to facilitate and monitor the implementation of the Framework Convention on Tobacco Control, in 2008 WHO introduced a number of MPOWER measures. These include:

- monitoring tobacco use and prevention policies;

- protecting people from tobacco use;

- offering help to quit tobacco use;

- warning about the dangers of tobacco;

- enforcing bans on tobacco advertising, promotion and sponsorship;

- raising taxes on tobacco.

In the development and implementation of these tobacco controls, WHO (2012a) has noted the importance of monitoring and examining those who have sought to oppose the implementation of these measures – namely the tobacco industry. The interests of the tobacco industry can be seen as securing the cost effectiveness of growing and sourcing material, most notably tobacco leaf, along with the production and transport of goods, in addition to access to sizeable markets. Clearly, the measures recommended by WHO present a threat to these interests and it is the strategies and practices undertaken by the tobacco industry as a corporate policy actor in defence of these interests that will now be discussed.

Although there are some seminal works that have sought to examine and articulate relations between 'capital', the state and policy (Holloway and Picciotto, 1978; Jessop, 1990; Miliband, 1973; O'Connor, 1973) relatively less attention has been paid to the specific strategies and practices of corporate actors in the problem policy process. Notable exceptions to this include Baggott (2006), Givel and Glantz (2001), Holden and Lee (2009), Farnsworth and Holden (2006) and Miller and Mooney (2010). For the purposes of this discussion, Farnsworth and Holden (2006) provide a conceptual framework for the analysis of the role and influence of corporate power on the problem policy process. An important part of this framework is the analytical distinction to be drawn between 'structural' and 'agency' power.

Structural power is used to describe policy makers' (in this instance, a national government) anticipation of corporate needs and demands, rather than the actual acts of corporations. Structural power is epitomised in the potential of corporations to take flight if governments enact policies that are considered to be harmful to the corporation's interests. This can be considered a form of direct action. The structural power of the tobacco industry can be enhanced by reducing the entry of new companies into the marketplace (Holden and Lee, 2009). In this regard, a number of entry barriers (Shepherd, 1985) and predatory actions against newcomers (Adams and Brock, 1998) have appeared to maintain the dominance of the big four transnational tobacco companies (Holden and Lee, 2009). Structural power is also enhanced when a national economy is seen to benefit from the presence of the tobacco companies – particularly with regard to the farming of tobacco leaf. Although only a small number of national economies may be over-reliant on tobacco farming as a source of income, in those countries, the impact of any anticipated departure by the tobacco company may lead the respective government to anticipate and meet the needs of the industry. This may include ensuring that favourable conditions for production, distribution and export are met, and a reduced enthusiasm for introducing tobacco controls.

In contrast, corporate agency reflects those instances where corporations do act. This corporate agency can take three broad and at times overlapping forms with regard to attempts to influence the problem policy process.

○ Direct provision and production – corporations are directly involved in the provision of services. This may be health or financial insurance companies or companies contracted to perform public services and other companies offering 'backroom' services.

o Institutional participation – senior figures and representations from corporations take positions on governmental bodies, eg quangos (quasi autonomous non-governmental organisations), government reports, commissions and inquiries. The use of government tsars to address particular issues, eg 'drug tsar', 'business tsar', is a notable example of members of corporations occupying a pivotal position in the problem policy process.

o Political engagements – lobbying and networking with the politicians and other policy actors; sponsoring and funding of research and think tanks, professorial chairs that are then charged with the remit of informing debates.

It is the tobacco industry's use of agency, most notably political engagement, that is of particular interest here. This agency has been exhibited at a global and national level. Holden and Lee (2009), drawing on internal industry documents released following litigation in the USA in the 1990s, identified the use of:

o contract lobbyists;

o campaign contributions to legislators;

o contributions to political caucuses and political parties;

o 'gifts', honoraria and the use of corporate hospitality;

o charitable donations;

o alliances with other interest groups and the use of 'front' groups, eg bogus hotel and restaurant associations, to influence state legislation.

A sustained and expensive campaign was launched by the tobacco companies. An estimated total of $170 million dollars was spent on professional lobbying firms and in-house lobbyists in an attempt to influence the US congress between 1999 and 2007 (TFK, 2007). Political donations to federal candidates, national parties and non-party political action committees (PACs) totalled more than

$34.7million during the years 1997–2007 (TFK, 2007). Indirect measures included attempts to challenge and undermine the evidence and arguments of those supporting tobacco controls. This has taken the form of organisations such as the Council for Tobacco Research (CTR), formed in 1954. Although purportedly an independent institute, the industry's own internal documents suggest the CTR also sought to cast doubt on the link between smoking and lung cancer (Bero, 2003).

What is notable is that as the context for the problem policy process has changed, so has the position, strategies and practices employed by the tobacco industry as an actor within that process. The enactment of the WHO Framework Convention on Tobacco Control may suggest that the tobacco industry's efforts have been in vain and the potential of the industry to act has been reduced. However, an era of trade liberalisation has provided new opportunities and challenges for both the relevant corporate actors and public health agencies as they continue the struggle over the production, distribution and consumption of tobacco and seek to establish agreement as to the right balance between trade, investment and health (WHO, 2012b).

THE PIQUETEROS

In Argentina, the origins of what came to be described as the piqueteros, a mobilisation of the unemployed, can be found in the oil towns of Cutral-Co, Plaza Huincul, General Mosconi and Tartagal in 1996 and 1997 (Wolff, 2007). Defined through the use of *piquetes* – roadblocks – the piqueteros soon not only became prominent actors on the national stage, but also gained international renown. The term piquete may have been used in Argentina since the end of the nineteenth century to describe unemployed people's blockades of factories, workshops and other establishments, but in 1996 the word took on a new contemporary resonance as the piqueteros started to take direct action.

The first acts were to be found in the context of the privatisation of the state petroleum company Yacimientos Petroliferos Fiscales

(YPF), significant job losses and the relative absence of alternative work opportunities and social and welfare support. Tactics and ideas varied across and within the various groupings of piqueteros, but direct action, particularly the use of blockades, remained a potent intervention. The blockades were organised through word of mouth and the distribution of posters and flyers citing the date, place and time to block roads to stop the transportation of goods. Materials that were readily to hand, most notably tyres and the people themselves, were used to form the barricades. Foreshadowing the Occupy movement, tents and makeshift kitchens were established alongside the blockades. The sight of hundreds, sometimes thousands, of people at a bridge, main road or town centre not only caused the necessary disruptions and brought the scale of the problem into view, but also, despite concerted efforts on the part of the authorities, limited the effectiveness of the use of force in efforts to move the protestors on.

The use of roadblocks in these towns and cities, despite attempts to suppress them, led to disruptions of transport and industry which effectively forced representatives from the state to hear and negotiate with the piqueteros. These early actions appeared to provide a model for other piqueteros across the country. Characterised by open assemblies and participatory forms of self-organisation, and constituted by the unemployed from squatter settlements and a number of suburban and urban locations, by the end of 1997, the use of 170 piquetes had been recorded. The number of piquetes in evidence quickly increased. Some of the numbers are disputed but, between 1997 and 2004, it is estimated that the total number of road blocks was 7,135, an average of 892 per year (Ronconi and Franceschelli, 2007, p 288). The result of such actions was that the piqueteros became, for a short time at least, a robust and influential political actor on the national scene.

So why did the piqueteros mobilise at this time? In the 1990s, Argentina was subject to mass unemployment and under-employment and increasing levels of poverty. Then it experienced a financial and political context that saw national unemployment figures of around 30 per cent in 1995 and 37.7 per cent in October

2002 (Auyero, 2001; Epstein, 2006). However, the existence of inequalities, poverty and social deprivation does not necessarily translate into campaigns, protests and practices that seek to address such issues. One explanation offered is that previously and newly marginalised groups were able not only to identify a means of exercising power, but also to use this new-found influence to win material concessions. More specifically, the disruptive potential offered through the use of roadblocks enabled the piqueteros to win concessions from the state, namely what were described as *planes socials* – social subsidies granted to unemployed households for the purposes of supporting municipal work schemes and local development projects (Benclowicz, 2010; Dinerstein, 2001). Arguably an extension of the practice of *political clientelism, where goods and services are traded for political favours* (Auyero, 2001), these relatively modest forms of financial support, combined with the solidarity and voice that such activities realised (Sitrin, 2006) also helped sustain the piqueteros.

However, it should also be noted that the piqueteros did not just spontaneously emerge. The relations and practices that characterised them can be considered to have their origins in the poor's *retreat to the barrio* (Wolff, 2007). In the absence of state and corporate forms of support and a weakened labour movement, as is the case in a number of the world's fast-growing global cities, the unemployed, under-employed and self-employed took it upon themselves to occupy land and provide shelter and basic amenities (Davis, 2007). It was this self-organisation and the networks that serviced them that provided the schooling for the relations and practices of the piqueteros (Sitrin, 2006; Wolff, 2007).

The piqueteros were far from the only social or labour movement that was responsible for social protests and campaigns during the financial and political crises of this period. However, what is notable about them was not just the tactics used – open assemblies and roadblocks – but that it was a movement constituted by those normally considered excluded and marginal to the political and policy process (Abal Medina, 2010). Other groups and parties may have sought to represent such constituencies in the past, and continue to do so (Dinerstein, 2010). However, when such representation, if not the political and policy system as a whole, was found wanting, the piqueteros sought to represent themselves.

CONCLUSION

It is beyond the scope and focus of this chapter to discuss the merits or otherwise of the policies and practices described in these accounts. Rather, it is the role of the policy actors and their assumptions in shaping the problem policy process that is of interest. For example, despite the apparent rationality and evidence offered by the social reformers and campaigners for the 'feeble-minded', the alleged residuum, of which the mentally defective were considered to be a part, may be best understood as a 'phantom army' conjured by some of those social researchers, scientists and reformers of the period in order to legitimate their own practices and proposals. Far from being the result of biology or moral failing, the *unemployable* and *irredeemable* appeared to become both employable and redeemable once work opportunities became available. As such, it appeared to be poorhouses, wages and the irregular work of *darkest England* that provided the conditions for the alleged residuum to *thrive* (Stedman-Jones, 1984). Similarly, the social investigators, commentators and reformers may well have intended to operate in the best interests of the 'feeble-minded', but it is notable that, in light of the threat that this group was considered to pose to the health of the nation, the resulting legislation was *willing to sacrifice the interests of these individuals when this was thought to be in the interests of the wider community* (Harris, 2004, p 165). Finally, it should also be noted that the identification and treatment of *problem groups* proved to be a persuasive argument. The corralling of the feeble-minded appeared to offer a solution to a range of social problems without requiring a change to existing social, political and economic relations (MacNicol, 1983, p 177–78).

A more obvious, if until relatively recently less visible, facet of a policy actor's position is revealed through the case of tobacco control. However, it is not just the pursuit of an agenda by the tobacco industry that is of interest, but also what the account reveals about attempts to shape the rules of the game. The communication strategies and lobbying employed by the tobacco industry can be seen as seeking to exert influence on the problem policy process, as well as being engaged in the reshaping of the infrastructure and processes of the problem policy process. In other words, the rules and regulations within which democracy, politics and the economy operate have not only been influenced, but arguably captured by lobbying for sectional interests. Lobbying has been – in other words – one of the midwives of contemporary policy and politics (Miller and Dinan, 2008). However, before the problem policy process is considered the sole domain of powerful interest groups, the piqueteros provide an instructive case study in how such assumptions and practices can be interrupted. The absence of orthodox forms of party organisation and discipline among the various strands and groups of piqueteros might have proved to be an obstacle when seeking to move into more formal and orthodox political and policy spaces. Similarly, the scale and nature of the concessions that were won and the relatively quick taming of the movement might bring us to question whether the piqueteros provide a desirable or sustainable model for social, political and economic change. However, it is notable that despite charges that they failed to resolve deep political and strategic differences within the movement, its potential to disrupt and exercise power over the problem policy process was not blunted. Operating under the slogan *Que se vayan todos* – 'Out with them all!' (Wolff, 2007), the piqueteros made use of the resources available to them not only to demand attention and win concessions but also to demonstrate that, if nothing else, they were no longer willing to adapt to the new reality, but sought to shape their own circumstances. As a result, successive governments have had to rethink their strategies and policies and have been *forced to invent new ways of guaranteeing the reproduction of the social order* (Abal Medina, 2010, p 88).

Conclusion

An intellectual? Yes. And never deny it. An intellectual is someone
whose mind watches itself. I like this, because I am happy to be
both halves, the watcher and the watched. 'Can they be brought
together?' This is a practical question. We must get down to it.
'I despise intelligence' really means: 'I cannot bear my doubts.'

Albert Camus, *Notebooks* (1935–42)

The position that has been reflected in this book is that rather than
start from the assumption that social problems and subsequent
policies reflect an inevitable response to pre-existing givens,
attention needs to be paid to how a 'problem' is fabricated and
how a particular response to a 'problem' is legitimated and enacted
(Bacchi, 1999, 2009; Best, 2008; Simpson and Connor, 2011). It has
been argued that this struggle over the meaning and response to a
range of social problems takes place not only in distant discussions
and institutions, but also as part of the fabric of everyday life. Put
another way, policies do not just impact on people, but people can
and should also have an impact on policies. To this end, this book
has sought to identify how to read and understand existing policies,
and also hopes to play a part in further developing the potential of
individuals, groups and institutions to write and perform their part
in the problem policy process.

Section 1 sought to further develop your capacity to read policy and
to better appreciate the position of others. By examining the types
of explanations that are available for understanding social problems
and their associated critiques, considering the role of categories
in understanding problems and policy and the role of policies in
creating and sustaining categories, and then reviewing the use of
legitimating practices, it is hoped that you are not only better able to
understand how particular understandings of problems and policies
are shaped, but, when placed within a wider context, to examine the
role of these practices in wider social and political struggles (van

Dijk, 1993, 1998; Fairclough, 2003; Jessop, 2004; van Leeuwen, 2005; Marston, 2000, 2004). In this respect, the use of the term critical is used not to denote a particular method or technique, but to signal that the work is undertaken as part of a project that is rooted in a radical critique of social relations (Billig, 2000, 2003). An attempt is made to unsettle the taken-for-granted suppositions and meanings of policy in order to identify particular threads to be followed that may present possibilities for reconstructing social action.

Section 2 sought to identify the parameters and outline some of the resources and approaches available for identifying and then communicating your own position as a policy actor. In this respect, Section 2 sought to provide an account of what could or should be done and the evidence and criteria to be considered when judging the value of such proposals. Chapter 4 described the nature and role of policy analysis, where a number of potential roles, namely the scholar, technician and advocate were examined. The aims, assumptions and methods employed in these different forms of policy analysis were discussed and the criteria by which the work undertaken by these different forms of policy analysis can and should be judged were examined. Chapter 5 asked questions about what is considered a good individual and society, and how the ethics of a policy actor's intent, actions and outcomes should be assessed when engaging in the problem policy process. Finally in Section 2, the aim of Chapter 6 was to consider the role and significance of communication when writing policy. Particular attention was paid to the assumptions and role of framing in the problem policy process, the intention being to facilitate the reader's own attempts to communicate their own position when writing policy.

In Section 3 the main aim was to examine how it is possible to go beyond the analysis of social problems and policies and to develop the potential to influence and shape the problem policy process. In Chapter 7, a number of models for understanding the problem policy process were outlined, namely the expert model, the deliberative model and the crisis model of policy making. The assumptions regarding the nature of policy making and what are regarded as the key relations, processes and actors in each of these models were discussed. In Chapter 8, four different dimensions of power were considered, where once again the emphasis was on identifying the assumptions that inform each dimension and the implications for those policy actors seeking to develop their potential to perform policy. Finally, in Chapter 9, three accounts of actions that have been taken by a range of policy actors in an attempt to influence and shape the problem policy process were outlined. In each of these accounts, attention was drawn to the diversity and range of policy actors, positions, practices, relations and sites of actions that constitute the problem policy process. Most notable in the context of this book, was a consideration of the relationship between taking action and the values, assumptions and interests that are reflected and realised through these actions.

When writing a text of this nature, one of the biggest considerations is the breadth of material to be covered and the depth at which such material should be examined. This book is a little idiosyncratic. With respect to breadth of study, in some respects it covers far more ground than a number of similar texts that promise an introduction to understanding social policy (eg performing policy) while at the same time neglecting what are arguably the fundamentals of social policy – accounts of key institutions, history of social policy and discussions of key concepts and theories. Similarly, with respect to depth, some topics have been discussed in more depth than one might expect (eg language, rhetoric and framing), whereas some of the material might be considered to have been given relatively scant attention (eg topics of need, risk and deservingness). Reflecting on these choices, it is clear that the aim of the book is not to replicate some of the excellent texts on social policy cited throughout, but to provide a different way of engaging in the problem policy process – namely to write a text from the position of a policy actor. Similarly, the book is not intended to be comprehensive, or to offer a particular way of understanding social policy, but to provide a number of different potential points of departure for engaging in the problem policy process. This is the challenge for a book of this nature. That is, it is envisaged that whatever your current potential and position with regard to the problem policy process, this book will help you further develop that potential and, if necessary, help you review, challenge and further your own position. It is for this reason that the book has sought to restrict the occasions when the reader is told what their position is or should be or how the reader should engage in the policy process. Put another way, rather than telling you what to think and how to act, the emphasis has been placed on attempting to consider how you think, and how to consider and communicate a position and the assumptions that underpin attempts to perform policy. However, clearly there are assumptions and recurrent themes that run throughout this book, so in case it is not apparent already, we conclude with a statement of the position that this book reflects and has sought to realise.

A VIEW FROM NOWHERE?

A recurrent theme in this book is the possibility and desirability of a view from nowhere – knowledge that is independent of, or does not reflect, a particular perspective. What the book argues is that, particularly when it comes to questions regarding the problem policy process, it is better to recognise that any view that is provided is from somewhere. This also requires you to consider the different perspectives that are available and the consequences of this multiple vantage point for examining the claims that are made in the problem policy process. This presents a significant challenge to anyone seeking to make sense of the claims that are made regarding problems and policy. However, there is a relatively everyday example that helps illustrate what is required. If you have ever used Google Maps (other map apps are available) you will know that it is possible to use 'street view', where you are on the ground and able to see and, with some restrictions, explore your immediate surroundings. This is closest to our everyday view of the world and the perspective of those delivering and in receipt of policies and services. The perspective tends to prioritise particular forms of knowledge and makes available particular forms of information as we seek to navigate the world at this level. The emphasis will be on what we need to do now. To arrive at our destination, we might not feel as though we need to know anything more than whether we should turn left, right or go straight ahead at the end of the street. Of course, it is possible to embellish these immediate surroundings with more information, eg who lives at the various addresses, how their homes are furnished, what the menu is at the local cafe, what reviews it has received, and whether there are any significant landmarks and information regarding the history of this place. We can continue collecting and identifying such information, but this information is organised, orientated and reflects a particular point of view.

However in street view, it is difficult to see where you are in relation to the streets around you, never mind the wider village, town, city and region. Fortunately, in Google Maps it is also possible to zoom out from street view, to various degrees of abstraction, until we are able to gain the perspective from a satellite and choose to see the world from afar. This may not reflect an everyday or immediate point of view, but from this lofty position it is now possible to see our original position in relation to the surrounding areas. Patterns previously hidden may now come into view and the irregularities and nature of the landscape as a whole become a great deal clearer. This is the perspective of orthodox forms of policy makers and analysts. The emphasis is placed on getting the bigger picture, while the details and distinctions that were gained from street view now become lost.

Admittedly, this description of the practitioner/service user perspective and the policy maker perspective may be caricatured, but it serves the purpose of illustrating how the different positions may have different needs and priorities as to what is required when understanding the problem policy process and the tensions that can exist when translating policy into practice. In this book, it is argued that both viewpoints have a purpose, so it would be wrong to privilege one over the other, and that therefore it is advantageous to appreciate what each perspective can offer. That is, it is good to recognise the position of those acting in the here and now, while also recognising our part in the bigger picture. Put another way, it is useful to understand how problems present themselves to individuals, and how those individuals' positions contribute to how they make sense of these problems, while also to seeking to understand the place of these individual practices within the dynamics and relations across the landscape as a whole.

REFLEXIVE POLICY PRAXIS

Given the complexity, uncertainty and unfolding nature of the problem policy process, at least as described in this book, the possibility of being overwhelmed and a desire to secure and hold on to a point of certainty is understandable. However, it is argued that rather than anchor praxis according to some external authority, what is considered vital to policy praxis is reflexivity. At its simplest this is understood as an understanding of the policy actor's practices, position, role and influence in the problem policy process. However, reflexivity is more than a reflection (Gergen, 1993). For example, imagine looking at a photograph of a younger version of yourself. The photograph may lead to a reflection on how different you looked and felt. Now if that photograph was particularly embarrassing in terms of hairstyle and dress, this might lead you to consider, what was I thinking? Why did I dress that way and have that haircut? If you go on to compare and contrast your look and attitude then with your look and attitude today, and ask how and why there may be differences, then you are beginning to exhibit reflexivity. However, reflexivity is more than 'looking back', it is also about anticipating, attending to and then responding to your own practices and the practices of others. Reflexivity is also more than a rationalisation of a policy actor's actions, that is, the reasons they may give for their actions if asked. Reflexivity extends this rationalisation to include a consciousness of the policy actor's practices, position, role, settings and intended and unintended consequences of their actions (Giddens, 1984; Gouldner, 1970; Hoggett, Jeffers and Harrison, 1994, p 69).

The contingency that has been highlighted throughout this book emphasises the dynamic and non-foundational characteristics of policy praxis. Interpretations are inevitable and these interpretations are specific to time, place and conditions (Strauss and Corbin, 1994, p 279). From this perspective, any knowledge, understanding or foundation for practice is considered not only contingent, but also a reflection of the policy actor's position. A logical extension of such a viewpoint is that if practice is context dependent and bound up with interests, then there is no way of making judgements about the legitimacy of different positions. Furthermore, an alleged rejection of objectivity may be considered an opportunity for the problem policy process to be occupied by 'fallacious', dubious and irrational policy actors. Consequently, in a world of indeterminate 'objectivity' there exists the potential for those with power to exploit this forum by 'marketing' certain viewpoints thereby reinforcing their position (Rosenau, 1992).

Furthermore, what is implied in the criticisms levelled at a relativistic position is the charge of impoverished debate, the argument being that if there is no basis for criticism, there is no room for debate (Luper, 2004). This assumes that ultimately in order to judge a theory correct or incorrect, good or bad, the existence of some universal, objective standard of merit is required. However, in the context of this book, rather than stifling discussion due to the lack of independent foundational criteria, the doubt that results from a contingent notion of knowledge is considered to lead to an enriched deliberative process. This is because there appears to be little room for debate when a set of immutable standards are established. Instead, recognition of the contingency of practice encourages the challenging and reaffirmation of what is to be held most sacred or most horrid. In this respect, although a desire for ontological security may be understandable, in the public realm at least, it is not required. Rather, doubt and contingency heighten the need for debate and attention to the 'social' foundations of society and its practices. This is an issue of particular relevance to the problem policy process, where a policy actor operating in a reflexive manner questions the assumptions that are made through their own praxis, the problem policy process as a whole and those assumptions related to the policy actor's social position (Hoggett, Jeffers and Harrison, 1994). As such, a reflexive policy actor is willing not only to reflect but reconsider and, if necessary, change their position through their practices (Dryzek, 2000). This book and the emphasis that has been placed on the different ways of reading, writing and performing policy has sought to facilitate a policy actor's potential to engage in a reflexive policy praxis.

An open deliberative problem policy process populated by reflexive policy actors may well be something to aspire to, but it should not necessarily be assumed. Distinct asymmetries in the potential to engage in the problem policy process may be in evidence. Each model of the problem policy process may make different assumptions regarding the nature, extent and impact of these asymmetries, but they all suggest that such differences exist, even if they differ with respect to the desirability or otherwise of such asymmetry. Furthermore, the book has sought to highlight how, at the heart of any attempt to understand and engage in the problem policy process, there is a struggle over access to the (re)production, distribution and consumption of resources. There may be different approaches to how such resources can and should be distributed and how any potential conflict or tensions can be resolved or responded to, but at no point is the struggle denied. In this regard, the problem policy process is a reflection and realisation of particular positions and as such it is both the site and vehicle for a struggle over how we can and should lead our lives. Some policy actors may seek to maintain the existing social, political and economic relations, while others may seek to modify, if not transform, those positions, relations and practices.

Having outlined a number of strategies and methods for engaging in the problem policy process, rather than closing down the scope of study, the book has sought to open up the parameters of what counts as policy praxis. Furthermore, rather than state what you should see, think and do, the book has sought to draw your attention to different ways of reading, writing and performing the problem policy process. In this respect, the book has been written not just for those new to the subject, but also to provide an aide memoire and a collection of heuristic devices for those embedded in the problem policy process and seeking to make sense of their current position and identify what direction to take. The onus is placed on the reader to choose for themselves how they should read, write and perform in the problem policy process. Arguably, such a choice could and should be informed through an explication and understanding of the reader's current position, as reflected in the book's title, *What's Your Problem?*. If nothing else, the book has aimed to show that when answering such a question, no policy actors should necessarily rely on others' accounts of what their problem is.

> The welfare of the people in particular has always been the alibi of tyrants, and it provides the further advantage of giving the servants of tyranny a good conscience. It would be easy, however, to destroy that good conscience by shouting to them: if you want the happiness of the people, let them speak out and tell what kind of happiness they want and what kind they don't want! But, in truth, the very ones who make use of such alibis know they are lies; they leave to their intellectuals on duty the chore of believing in them and of proving that religion, patriotism, and justice need for their survival the sacrifice of freedom. Camus (1961)

In summary, in the absence of an external authority, the challenge is to work through and fabricate your own response to the question, 'what is your problem?' and the equally vital inquiry, 'what are you going to do about it?'.

References

Abal Medina, P. (2011) *Thoughts on the Visual Aspect of the Neoliberal Order and the Piquetero Movement in Argentina. Latin American Perspectives*, 38(1): 88–101.

Adams, W. and Brock, J.W. (1998) Tobacco: Predation and Persistent Market Power, in Rosenbaum, D.I. (ed) *Market Dominance: How Firms Gain, Hold or Lose It and the Impact on Economic Performance.* WestPort, CT: Praeger.

Alinsky, S.D. (1946) *Reveille for Radicals.* New York: Random House.

Alinsky, S.D. (1971) *Rules for Radicals: A Pragmatic Primer for Realistic Radicals.* New York: Vintage.

Allison, G.T. (1971) *Essence of Decision: Explaining the Cuban Missile Crisis.* Boston, MA: Little Brown.

Althusser, L. (1971) *Lenin and Philosophy and Other Essays.* Translated by B. Brewster. London: Monthly Review Press.

Apthorpe, R. and Gasper, D. (eds) (1996) *Arguing Development Policy: Frames and Discourses. Introduction: Discourse Analysis and Policy Discourse.* London: Frank Cass.

Arendt, H. (1970) On Violence. London: Allen Lane.

Aristotle (*c.*350BC/1959) *The Art of Rhetoric.* Translated by J. H. Freese. Cambridge, MA: Harvard University Press.

Arora, P. (2012) Typology of Web 2.0 Spheres: Understanding the Cultural Dimensions of Social Media Spaces. *Current Sociology*, 60(5): 599–618.

Audi, R. (2011) *Epistemology: A Contemporary Introduction to the Theory of Knowledge*, 3rd edn. New York: Routledge.

Auyero, J. (2001) *Poor People's Politics: Peronist Survival Networks and the Legacy of Evita.* Durham and London: Duke University Press.

Bacchi, C. (1999) *Women, Policy and Politics.* London: Sage.

Bacchi, C. (2009) *Analysing Policy: What's the problem represented to be?* Frenchs Forest, NSW: Pearson.

Bacchi, C. (2012) Why Study Problematizations? Making Politics Visible. *Open Journal of Political Science*, 2(1): 1–8.

Bachrach, P. and Baratz, M.S. (1962) Two Faces of Power. *American Political Science Review*, 56(4): 947–52.

Baggini, J. (2002) *Philosophy: Key Themes.* Basingstoke: Palgrave Macmillan.

Baggott, R. (2006) *Alcohol Strategy and the Drinks Industry: A Partnership for Prevention?* York: Joseph Rowntree Foundation.

Bakhtin, M.M. (1986) *Speech Genres and Other Late Essays.* Edited by M. Holquist and C. Emerson, translated by V.W. McGee. Austin, TX: University of Texas Press.

Banks, S. (2012) *Ethics and Values in Social Work*, 4th edn. Basingstoke: Palgrave Macmillan.

Banks, S. and Gallagher, A. (2009) *Ethics in Professional Life: Virtues for Health and Social Care.* Basingstoke: Palgrave Macmillan.

Baptist, W. and Bricker-Jones, M. (2001) A View From the Bottom: People and Their Allies Respond to Welfare Reform. *The Annals of the Academy of Political and Social Science*, 577: 144–56.

Barnes, C. (1991) *Disabled People in Britain and Discrimination: A Case* for Anti- Discrimination Legislation. London: Hurst.

Barnes, M. and Prior, D. (eds) (2009) *Subversive Citizens: Power, Agency and Resistance in Public Services*. Bristol: Policy Press.

Baron, M.W., Pettit, P. and Slote, M. (1997) *Three Methods of Ethics*. Oxford: Blackwell.

Baron, M.W., Pettit, P. and Slote, M. (2008) *Three Methods of Ethics*. Oxford: Blackwell.

Bauman, Z. (1991) *Modernity and Ambivalence*. Oxford: Polity.

Bauman, Z. (2004) *Wasted Lives: Modernity and Its Outcasts*. Oxford: Polity.

Baumgartner, F.R. and Jones, B.D. (1993) *Agendas and Instability in American Politics*. Chicago, IL: University of Chicago Press.

Beck, D. and Purcell, R. (2013) *International Community Organising: Taking Power, Making Change*. Bristol: Policy Press.

Becker, H.A. (1967) *Introduction to Social Problems: A Modern Approach*. New York: John Wiley.

Béland, D. (2005) Ideas and Social Policy: An Institutionalist Perspective. *Social Policy & Administration*, 39(1): 1–18.

Bell, F. (1907) *At the Works: A Study of a Manufacturing Town*. London: Edward Arnold.

Benclowicz, J.D. (2010) Continuities, Scope, and Limitations of the Argentine Piquetero Movement: The Cases of Tartagal and Moscon. *Latin American Perspective*, 38(1): 74–87.

Benford, R.D. and Snow, D.A. (2000) Framing Processes and Social Movements: An Overview and Assessment. *Annual Review of Sociology*, 26: 611–39.

Bentham, J. (1789/1996) *An Introduction to the Principles of Morals and Legislation: An Authoritative Edition* by J.H. Burns and H.L.A. Hart; with a new introduction by F. Rosen and an interpretive essay by H.L.A. Hart. Oxford: Oxford University Press.

Beresford, P. and Holden, C. (2000) We Have Choices: Globalisation and Welfare User Movements. *Disability Society*, 15(7), 973–989.

Berger, P. and Luckmann, T. (1967) *The Social Construction of Reality*. London: Allen Lane.

Berlin, I. (1969) *Four Essays on Liberty*. Oxford: Oxford University Press.

Bernstein, R.J. (1976) *The Restructuring of Social and Political Theory*. Philadelphia, PA: University of Pennsylvania Press.

Bernstein, R.J. (1983) *Beyond Objectivism and Relativism: Science, Hermeneutics and Praxis*. Philadelphia, PA: University of Pennsylvania Press.

Bero, L. (2003) Implications of the Tobacco Industry Documents for Public Health and Policy. *Annual Review of Public Health*, 24: 267–88.

Best, J. (2008) *Social Problems*. London: W.W. Norton & Company.

Bevir, M. and Rhodes, R.A.W. (2003) *Interpreting British Governance*. London: Routledge.

Billig, M. (2000) Towards a Critique of the Critical. *Discourse & Society*, 11: 291–92.

Billig, M. (2003) Critical Discourse Analysis and the Rhetoric of Critique, in Weiss, G. and Wodak, R. (eds) *Critical Discourse Analysis*. London: Palgrave Macmillan.

Booth, W. (1890) *In Darkest England and the Way Out*. London: Project Gutenberg.

Boris, E. (2007) On Cowboys and Welfare Queens: Independence, Dependence, and Interdependence at Home and Abroad. *Journal of American Studies*, 41(3): 599–621.

Bosanquet, H. (1902) *The Strength of the People: A Study in Social Economics*. London: Messrs. Macmillan & Co.

Bostock, D. (2000) *Aristotle's Ethics*. Oxford: Oxford University Press.

Bourdieu, P. and Wacquant, L. (2001) New-Liberal Speak: Notes on the New Planetary Vulgate. *Radical Philosophy*, 105: 2–5.

Boykoff, J. and Laschever, E. (2011) The Tea Party Movement, Framing, and the US Media. *Social Movement Studies, 2011*, 10(4): 341–66.

Brah, A. (1996) *Cartographies of Diaspora: Contesting Identities*. London: Routledge.

Brewer, P.R. and Gross, K. (2005) Values, Framing, and Citizens' Thoughts About Policy Issues: Effects on Content and Quantity. *Political Psychology*, 26: 929–48.

Bridgman, P. and Davis, G. (2000) *Australian Policy Handbook*, 2nd edn. Sydney: Allen and Unwin.

Bridgman, P. and Davis, G. (2003) What Use Is a Policy Cycle? Plenty, If the Aim Is Clear. *Australian Journal of Public Administration*, 62(3): 98–102.

Bryson, L. (1992) *Welfare and the State: Who Benefits?* Basingstoke: Macmillan.

Bulmer, M. (1982) *The Uses of Social Research: Social Investigation in Public Policy-Making*. London: George Allen & Unwin.

Burke, K. (1962) *A Grammar of Motives: And a Rhetoric of Motives*. New York: Meridian.

Burr, V. (1995) *An Introduction to Social Constructionism*. London: Routledge.

Butler, J. (2004) *Undoing Gender*. London: Routledge.

Byrne, D. (2005) *Social Exclusion*, 2nd edn. Buckingham: Open University Press.

Camus, A. (1961) *Resistance, Rebellion, and Death*. Translated and with an introduction by J. O'Brien. London: H. Hamilton.

Carr, W. and Kemmis, S. (1986) *Becoming Critical: Education, Knowledge, and Action Research*. London: Falmer Press.

Carter, A. (2005) Direct Action and Democracy Today. Cambridge: Polity.

Chafel, J.A. (1997) Societal Images of Poverty: Child and Adult Beliefs. *Youth Society*, 28(4): 432–63.

Chisholm, R.M. (1989) *Theory of Knowledge*, 3rd edn. London: Prentice Hall.

Clark, C. (2000) *Social Work Ethics: Politics, Principles and Practice*. Basingstoke: Palgrave.

Clarke, J. (2004) *Changing Welfare, Changing States: New Directions in Social Policy*. London: Sage.

Clarke, J. (2005) New Labour's Citizens: Activated, Empowered, Responsibilized, Abandoned? *Critical Social Policy*, 25(4): 447–63.

Clarke, J. and Cochrane, A. (1998) Social Construction of Social Problems, in Saraga, E. (ed) *Embodying the Social: Constructions of Difference*. London: Routledge and Open University Press.

Colebatch, H.K. (2005) Policy Analysis, Policy Practice and Political Science. *Australian Journal of Public Administration*, 64(3): 14–23.

Colebatch, H.K. (2006) What Work Makes Policy. *Policy Science*, 39: 309–21.

Connor, S. (2007) We're Onto You: A Critical Examination of the Department for Work and Pensions' 'Targeting Benefit Fraud' Campaign.

Critical Social Policy, 27(2): 231–52.

Connor, S. (2010) Promoting 'Employ Ability': The Changing Subject of Welfare Reform in the UK. *Critical Discourse Studies*, 7(1): 41–53.

Connor, S. and Huggins, R. (2010) The Technology and the Artefacts of Social Control – Monitoring Criminal and Anti-Social Behaviour Through and in Media Cultures, in Chriss, J. (ed) *Sociology of Crime, Law and Deviance*, vol 15, Social Control: Informal, Legal and Medical. Cambridge, MA: Emerald.

Cook, D. (2006) *Criminal and Social Justice*. London: Sage.

Couldry, N. and Curran, J. (eds) (2003) *Contesting Media Power: Alternative Media in a Networked World*. Oxford: Rowman and Littlefield.

Crawshaw, P. (2008) Implementing the New Scientific Spirit: A Response To de Leeuw *et al. Critical Public Health*, 18(2): 135–37.

Dahl, R. (1957) The Concept of Power. *Behavioural Science*, 2(3): 203–4.

Dahl, R. (1958) A Critique of the Ruling Elite Model. *American Political Science Review*, 58: 463–64.

Dahl, R. (1971) *Polyarchy: Participation and Opposition*. London: Yale University Press.

Dahlberg, L. and Siapera, E. (2007) *Radical Democracy and the Internet*. Basingstoke: Palgrave.

Daly, M. (2003) Governance and Social Policy. *Journal of Social Policy*, 32(1): 113–28.

Davis, M. (2007) *Planet of the Slums*. London: Verso.

Daviter, F. (2007) Policy Framing in the European Union. *Journal of European Public Policy*, 14(4): 654–66.

Day, R.J.F. (2005) From Hegemony to Affinity. *Cultural Studies*, 18(5): 716–48.

de Beauvoir, S. (1949/2010) *The Second Sex*. Translated by Constance Borde and Sheila Malovany-Chevallier. London: Vintage Books.

De Leeuw, E., McNess, A., Crisp, B. and Stagnitti, K. (2008) Theoretical Reflections on the Nexus Between Research, Policy and Practice. *Critical Public Health*, 18(1): 5–20.

Deacon, D. and Golding, P. (1994) *Taxation and Representation: The Media, Political Communication and the Poll Tax*. London: John Libbey.

Della Porta, D. and Tarrow, S. (eds) (2005) *Transnational Protest and Global Activism*. Oxford: Rowman & Littlefield.

Denzin, N.K. (1970) *The Research Act in Sociology*. London: Butterworth.

Dewey, J. (1927) *The Public and Its Problems*. New York: Holt.

Dinerstein, A. C. (2001) Roadblocks in Argentina: Against the Violence of Stability. *Capital & Class*, 25(2): 1–7.

Dinerstein, A.C. (2010) Autonomy in Latin America: Between Resistance and Integration. Echoes from the Piqueteros Experience. *Community Development Journal*, 45(3): 356–66.

Dodge, J. (2010) Tensions in Deliberative Practice: A View From Civil Society. *Critical Policy Studies*, 4(4): 384–404.

Doherty, B., Plows, A. and Wall, D. (2003) The Preferred Way of Doing Things: The British Direct Action Movement. *Parliamentary Affairs*, 56(4): 669–86.

Donnison, D. (1972) Research for Policy. *Minerva*, 10(4): 519–36.

Dowding, K. (1995) Model or Metaphor? A Critical Review on the

Policy Network Approach. *Political Studies*, 43(1): 136–58.

Dowding, K. (1996) *Power*. Buckingham: Open University Press.

Dowding, K. (2006) Three-Dimensional Power: A Discussion of Steven Lukes' Power: A Radical View. *Political Studies Review*, 4: 136–45.

Dror, Y. (1971) *Design for Policy Sciences*. New York: Elsevier.

Dryzek, J. S. (2000) *Deliberative Democracy and Beyond: Liberals, Critics and Contestations*. Oxford: Oxford University Press.

Dye, T. R. (1976) *Policy Analysis*. Alabama, AL: University of Alabama Press.

Edelman, M. (1977) *Political Language: Words That Succeed and Policies That Fail*. New York: Academic Press.

Edelman, M. (1988) *Constructing the Political Spectacle*. Chicago, IL: University of Chicago Press.

Edelman, M. (1995) *From Art to Politics: How Artistic Creations Shape Political Conceptions*. Chicago, IL: The University of Chicago Press.

Elias, N. (1969) *The Court Society*. Oxford: Basil Blackwell.

Elster, J. (1998) *Deliberative Democracy*. New York: Cambridge University Press.

Entman, R. (2004) *Projections of Power: Framing News, Public Opinion and Foreign Policy*. Chicago, IL: University of Chicago Press.

Epstein, E. (2006) The Piquetero Movement in Greater Buenos Aires: Political Protests by the Unemployed Poor During the Crisis, in Epstein, E. and Pion-Berlin, D. (eds) *Broken Promises? The Argentine Crisis and Argentine Democracy*. Plymouth: Lexington Books.

Fairclough, N. (1989) *Language and Power*. London: Longman.

Fairclough, N. (2000) *New Labour, New Language?* London: Routledge.

Fairclough, N. (2003) *Analyzing Discourse: Textual Analysis for Social Research*. London: Routledge.

Fairclough, N. and Fairclough, I. (2012) *Political Discourse Analysis*. London: Routledge.

Fanon, F. (1961/2004) *The Wretched of the Earth*. Translated by R. Philcox with commentary by J.-P. Sartre and H. K. Bhabha. New York: Gove Press.

Farnsworth, K. and Holden, C. (2006) The Business-Social Policy Nexus: Corporate Power and Corporate Inputs into Social Policy. *Journal of Social Policy*, 35(3): 471–94.

Farnsworth, K. and Irving, Z. (eds) (2011) *Social Policy in Challenging Times: Economic Crisis and Welfare Systems*. Bristol: The Policy Press.

Fawcett, P. and Daugbjerg, C. (2012) Explaining Governance Outcomes: Epistemology, Network Governance and Policy Network Analysis. *Political Studies Review*, 10(2): 195–207.

Fink, L., Leonard, S.T. and Reid, D.M. (eds) (1996) *Intellectuals and Public Life: Between Radicalism and Reform*. Ithaca and London: Cornell University Press.

Firestone, S. (1970/2003) *The Dialectic of Sex: The Case for Feminist Revolution*. New York: Farrar Straus Giroux.

Fischer, F. (2003) *Reframing Public Policy Discursive Politics and Deliberative Practices*. Oxford: Oxford University Press.

Fischer, F. and Gottweis, H. (eds) (2012) *The Argumentative Turn Revisited: Public Policy as Communicative Practice*. Durham, North Carolina: Duke University Press.

Fitzpatrick, T. (2005) *New Theories of Welfare*. Basingstoke: Palgrave Macmillan

Fitzpatrick, T. (2008) *Applied Ethics and Social Problems: Moral Questions of Birth, Society and Death*. Bristol: Policy Press.

Flyvbjerg, B. (2001) *Making Social Science Matter. Why Social Inquiry Fails and How It Can Succeed Again*. Cambridge: Cambridge University Press.

Flyvbjerg, B. Landman, T. and Schram, S. (eds) (2012) Real Social Science: Applied Phronesis. Cambridge: Cambridge University Press

Foley, R. (1998) Justification, Epistemic, in Craig, E. (ed) *Routledge Encyclopaedia of Philosophy*, vol 5, pp 157–65. London: Routledge.

Fornäs, J. (1995) *Cultural Theory and Late Modernity*. London: Sage.

Foucault, M. (1971) *Madness and Civilization: A History of Insanity in the Age of Reason*. London: Tavistock.

Foucault, M. (1980) *Power/Knowledge*. Brighton: Harvester Press.

Foucault, M. (1988) *The History of Sexuality*, vol 3 The Care of the Self. Translated by R. Hurley. London: Allen.

Foucault, M. (1990) *The History of Sexuality*, vol 1 The Will to Knowledge. Translated by R. Hurley. London: Penguin.

Foucault, M. (1992) *The History of Sexuality*, vol 2 The Use of Pleasure. Translated by R. Hurley. London: Penguin.

Frameworks Institute (n.d.) www.frameworksinstitute.org/mission.html.

Franklin, B. (2004) *Packaging Politics: Political Communications in Britain's Media Democracy*, 2nd edn. London: Arnold.

The Free Association (2011) *Moments of Excess. Movements, Protest and Everyday Life*. Oakland, CA: PM Press.

Fumerton, R. (2006) *Epistemology*. Malden, MA: Blackwell.

Gal, J. and Weiss-Fal, I. (2013) *Social Workers Affecting Social Policy. An International Perspective*. Bristol: Policy Press.

Gamson, W.A. (1992) *Talking Politics*. Cambridge: Cambridge University Press.

Gamson, W.A. and Wolsfeld, G. (1993) Movement and Media as Interacting Systems. *Annals of the American Academy of Political Science*, 528(1): 114–25.

Gandhi, M.K. (1962) *Gandhi on Non-violence: A Selection from the Writings of Mahatma Gandhi*. T. Merton (ed). New York: New Directions Publishing.

Gans, J.J. (1995) *The War Against the Poor: The Underclass and Antipoverty Policy*. New York: Basic Books.

George, V. and Wilding, P. (1993) *Welfare and Ideology*. London: Prentice Hall.

Gergen, K.J. (1993) *Toward Transformation in Social Knowledge*, 2nd edn. London: Sage.

Giddens, A. (1984) *The Constitution of Society*. Berkeley, CA: University of California Press.

Givel, M. and Glantz, S. (2001) Tobacco Lobby Political Influence on US State Legislatures in the 1990s. *Tobacco Control*, 10: 124–34.

Gordon, I., Lewis, J. and Young, K. (1977) *Perspective on Policy Analysis*. Kent: Urban and Regional Studies: University of Kent.

Gough, I. (1979) *The Political Economy of the Welfare State*. London: Macmillan.

Gough, I. and Doyal, L. (1991) *A Theory of Human Need*. New York: Guilford Press.

Gouldner, A.W. (1962) Anti-Minotaur: The Myth of a Value Free Sociology. *Social Problems*, 9: 199–213.

Gouldner, A.W. (1968) The Sociologist as Partisan. *American Sociologist*, 3(2): 103–16.

Gouldner, A.W. (1970) *The Coming Crisis of Western Sociology*. London: Heinemann.

Graham, P. (2001) Space: Irrealis Objects in Technology Policy and Their Role in a New Political Economy. *Discourse and Society*, 12(6): 761–88.

Gramsci, A. (2003) *Prison Notebooks: Selections*. London: Lawrence & Wishart Ltd.

Gray, M. (2010) Moral Sources and Emergent Ethical Theories in Social Work. *British Journal of Social Work*, 40: 1794–811.

Greene, J.C. (1990) Knowledge Accumulation: Three Views on the Nature and Role of Knowledge in Social Science, in Guba, E.G. (ed) *The Paradigm Dialog*. Newbury Park, CA: Sage.

Guba, E.G. (1990) The Alternative Paradigm Dialog, in Guba, E.G. (ed) *The Paradigm Dialog*. Newbury Park, CA: Sage.

Gubrium, J.F. and Silverman, D. (1989) *The Politics of Field Research – Sociology Beyond Enlightenment*. London: Sage.

Guetzkow, J. (2010) Beyond Deservingness: Congressional Discourse on Poverty, 1964–1996. *The Annals of the American Academy of Political and Social Science*, 629: 173–97.

Habermas, J. (1996) *Between Facts and Norms: Contributions to a Discourse Theory of Law and Democracy*. Cambridge, MA: MIT Press.

Hajer, M. (2003) Policy Without Polity: Policy Analysis and the Institutional Void. *Policy Sciences*, 36: 175–95.

Hall, P.A. (1993) Policy Paradigms, Social Learning and the State: The Case of Economic Policy-Making in Britain. *Comparative Politics*, 25: 175–96.

Ham, C. and Hill, M. (1984) *The Policy Process in the Modern Capitalist State*. Hemel Hempstead: Wheatsheaf.

Handler, J.F. and Hasenfeld, T. (1991) *The Moral Construction of Poverty: Welfare Reform in America*. Newbury Park, CA: Sage.

Hardt, M. and Negri, A. (2000) *Empire*. Cambridge, MA: Harvard University Press.

Harris, B. (2004) *The Origins of the British Welfare State: Social Welfare in England and Wales, 1800–1945*. Basingstoke: Palgrave Macmillan.

Harris, J. (1995) Between Civic Virtue and Social Darwinism: The Concept of the Residuum, in Englander, D. and O'Day, R. (eds) *Retrieved Riches: Social Investigation in Britain 1840–1914*. Aldershot: Scolar Press.

Hartsock, N. (1990) Foucault on Power, in Nicholson L. J. (ed) Feminism / Postmodernism. New York: Routledge.

Harvey, L. (1990) *Critical Social Research*. London: Unwin Hyman.

Hay, C. (1999) Crisis and the Structural Transformation of the State: Interrogating the Process of Change. *British Journal of Politics and International Relations*, 1(3): 317–44.

Hay, C. (2001) The Crisis of Keynesianism and the Rise of Neoliberalism in Britain: An Ideational Institutionalist Approach, in Campbell, J.L. and Pedersen, O.K. (eds) *The Rise of Neoliberalism and*

Institutional Analysis. Princeton, NJ: Princeton University Press.

Hay, C. (2012) Political Analysis. Basingstoke: Palgrave.

Hayek, F.A. (1944) *The Road to Serfdom*. London: Routledge and Kegan Paul.

Hayek, F.A. (1960) *The Constitution of Liberty*. London: Routledge and Kegan Paul.

Hayek, F.A. (1944/1991) *The Road to Serfdom*. London: Routledge.

Heclo, H. (1972) Review Article: Policy Analysis. *British Journal of Political Science*, 2(1): 83–108.

Heineman, R.A., Bluhm, W.T., Peterson, S.A. and Kearny, E.N. (2002) *The World of the Policy Analyst. Rationality, Values and Politics*. London: Chatham House Publishers.

Hennock, E.P. (1976) Poverty and Social Theory in England: The Experience of the Eighteen-Eighties. *Social History*, 1(1): 67–91.

Herman, B. (1993) The Practice of Moral Judgment. Cambridge, MA: Harvard University Press.

Herman, E. S. and Chomsky, N. (1988) *Manufacturing Consent: The Political Economy of the Mass Media*. New York: Pantheon Books.

Hill, M. (2005) *The Public Policy Process*, 4th edn. London: Pearson-Longman.

Hodgson, S.M. and Irving, Z. (eds) (2007) *Policy Reconsidered: Meanings, Politics and Practices*. Bristol: The Policy Press.

Hoggett, P., Jeffers, S. and Harrison, L. (1994) Reflexivity and Uncertainty in the Research Process. *Policy and Politics*, 22(1): 59–70.

Hogwood, B.W. and Gunn, L.A. (1984) *Policy Analysis for the Real World*. Oxford: Oxford University Press.

Holden, C. and Lee, K. (2009) Corporate Power and Social Policy: The Political Economy of Transnational Tobacco Companies. *Global Social Policy*, 9(3): 328–54.

Holloway, J. and Picciotto, S. (1978) *State and Capital: A Marxist Debate*. London: Edward Arnold.

Hood, C. (1998) *The Art of the State: Culture, Rhetoric, and Public Management*. Oxford: Clarendon.

Houston, S. (2003) Establishing Virtue in Social Work: A Response to McBeath and Webb. *British Journal of Social Work*, 33: 819–24.

Howarth, D. (2010) Power, Discourse and Policy: Articulating a Hegemony Approach to Critical Policy Studies. *Critical Policy Studies*, 3(3–4): 309–35.

Howarth, D. and Griggs, S. (2012) Poststructuralist Policy Analysis: Discourse, Hegemony and Critical Explanation, in Fischer, F. and Gottweiss, H. (eds) *The Argumentative Turn Revisited: Public Policy as Communicative Practice*. Durham and London: Duke University Press.

Howlett, M. and Ramesh, M. (2003) *Studying Public Policy: Policy Cycles and Policy Subsystems*. Oxford: Oxford University Press.

Hugman, R. (2005) *New Approaches in Ethics for the Caring Professions: Taking Account of Change for Caring Professions*. London: Palgrave Macmillan.

Isaac, J.C. (1987a) Beyond the Three Faces of Power: A Realist Critique. *Polity*, 20(1): 4–31.

Isaac, J.C. (1987b) Power and Marxist Theory: A Realist View. Ithaca, NY: Cornell University Press.

Iyengar, S. (1996) Framing Responsibility for Political Issues. *Annals of the American Academy of Political and Social Science*, 546: 59–70.

Janowitz, M. (1972) *Sociological Models and Social Policy*. Morristown, NJ: General Learning Systems.

Jessop, B. (1990) *State Theory. Putting the Capitalist State in Its Place*. Cambridge: Polity Press.

Jessop, B. (2004) Critical Semiotic Analysis and Cultural Political Economy. *Critical Discourse Studies*, 1(2): 159–74.

Jessop, B. (2009) Cultural Political Economy and Critical Policy Studies. *Critical Policy Studies*, 3(3–4): 336–56.

Jones, G. (1986) *Social Hygiene in the Twentieth Century*. London: Croom Helm.

Jones, O. (2011) *The Demonization of the Working Class*. London: Verso.

Jordan, B. (1998) *The New Politics of Welfare: Social Justice in a Global Context*. London: Sage.

Kant, I. (1781/1998) *Critique of Pure Reason*. Translated and edited by P. Guyer and A.W. Wood. Cambridge: Cambridge University Press.

Kant, I., (1785/2012) *Groundwork of the Metaphysic of Morals*. Translated and edited by M. Gregor and J. Timmermann; translation revised by J. Timmerman; with an introduction by C.M. Korsgaard. Cambridge: Cambridge University Press.

Kant, I. (1788/1997) *Critique of Practical Reason*. Translated and edited by M. Gregor, with an introduction by A. Reath. Cambridge: Cambridge University Press.

Kant, I. (1997) *Lectures on Ethics*. Edited by P. Heath and J. Schneewind, and translated by P. Heath. Cambridge: Cambridge University Press.

Katz, M.B. (1989) *The Undeserving 'Poor': From the War on Poverty to the War of Welfare*. New York: Pantheon Books.

Keating, P. (1976) *Into Unknown England, 1866–1913: Selections from the Social Explorers*. Manchester: Manchester University Press.

Keck, M.E. and Sikkink, K. (1998) *Activists Beyond Borders: Advocacy Networks in International Politics*. Ithaca, NY: Cornell University Press.

Kemshall, H. (2002) *Risk, Social Policy and Welfare*. Buckingham: Open University Press.

Kingdon, J. (2011) *Agendas, Alternatives, and Public Policies*, 2nd edn. London: Longman.

Kuhn, T.S. (1962) *The Structure of Scientific Revolutions*. Chicago, IL: University of Chicago Press.

Kuypers, J.A. (2009) *Rhetorical Criticism: Perspectives in Action*. Lanham, MD: Lexington Press.

Laclau, E. and Mouffe, C. (2001) *Hegemony and Socialist Strategy: Towards a Radical Democratic Politics*, 2nd edn. London: Verso.

Lakoff, G. (2004) *Don't Think of an Elephant: Know Your Values and Frame the Debate*. White River Junction, VT: Chelsea Green Publishing Company.

Larsen, C.A. and Andersen, J.G. (2009) How New Economic Ideas Changed the Danish Welfare State: The Case of Neoliberal Ideas and Highly Organized Social Democratic Interests. *Governance: An International Journal of Policy Administration and Institutions*, 22(2): 239–61.

Lasswell, H.D. (1950/1936) *Politics: Who Gets What, When and How*. New York: Peter Smith.

Lasswell, H.D. (1951) The Policy Orientation, in Lerner, D. and Lasswell, H. (eds) *The Policy Sciences*. Stanford, CA: Stanford University Press.

Ledwith, M. (2007) Reclaiming the Radical Agenda: A Critical Approach to Community Development. *Concept*, 17(2): 8–12.

Lemke, J. (1995) *Textual Politics*. London: Taylor & Francis.

Lens, V. (2005) Advocacy and Argumentation in the Public Arena: A Guide for Social Workers. *Social Work*, 50(3): 231–38.

Leonard, S.T. (1996) Introduction: A Genealogy of the Politicized Intellectual, in Fink, L., Leonard, S.T. and Reid, D.M. (eds) *Intellectuals and Public Life: Between Radicalism and Reform*. Ithaca and London: Cornell University Press.

Lindblom, C.E. (1959) The Science of Muddling Through. *Public Administration Review*, 19: 78–88.

Lister, R. (2004) *Poverty*. Cambridge: Polity.

Loane, M. (1910) *Neighbours and Friends*. London: Edward Arnold.

Lukacs, G. (1920/1971) *History and Class Consciousness: A Study in Marxist Dialectics*. Boston, MA: MIT Press.

Lukes, S. (1974) *Power: A Radical View*. London: Macmillan.

Luper, S. (2004) Epistemic Relativism. *Philosophical Issues*, 14, a supplement to Noûs: 271–95.

MacIntyre, A. (2007) *After Virtue: A Study in Moral Theory*, 3rd edn. London: Bristol Classic.

MacNicol, J. (1983) Eugenics, Medicine and Mental Deficiency: An Introduction. *Oxford Review of Education*, 9(3): 177–80.

Majone, G. (1989) *Evidence, Argument, and Persuasion in the Policy Process*. New Haven: Yale University Press.

Marsh, D. and Rhodes, R.A.W. (eds) (1992) *Policy Networks in British Government*. Oxford: Clarendon Press.

Marsh, D. and Smith, M. (2001) Debate: There is More than One Way to Do a Political Science: On Different Ways to Study Policy Networks. *Political Studies*, 49: 528–41.

Marshall, T.H. (1967) *Social Policy*, 2nd edn. London: Routledge and Kegan Paul.

Marston, G. (2000) Metaphor, Morality and Myth: A Critical Discourse Analysis of Public Housing Policy in Queensland. *Critical Social Policy*, 20(3): 349–74.

Marston, G. (2004) *Social Policy and Discourse Analysis: Policy Change in Public Housing*. Aldershot: Ashgate.

Martín Rojo, L. and van Dijk, T.A. (1997) There Was a Problem, and It Was Solved! Legitimating the Expulsion of 'Illegal' Immigrants in Spanish Parliamentary Discourse. *Discourse & Society*, 8(4): 523–67.

Marx, L. (1867/2005) *Capital*, vol I. London: Penguin.

Mayntz, R. (1976) Conceptual Models of Organizational Decision Making and Their Application to the Policy Process, in Hofstede, G. and Kassem, M.S. (eds) *European Contributions to Organisation Theory*. Amsterdam: Van Gorcum.

McBeath, G. and Webb, S. (2002) Virtue Ethics and Social Work: Being Lucky, Realistic, and not Doing One's Duty. *British Journal of Social Work*, 32: 1015–36.

McChesney, R.W. (2007) *Communication Revolution: Critical Junctures and the Future of Media*. London: New Press.

McKay, S. (2011) Response 1: Scientific Method in Social Policy Research Is Not a Lost Cause. *Journal of Social Policy*, (40)1: 21–29.

McLennan, G. (2011) *Story of Sociology: A First Companion to Social Theory*. London: Bloomsbury.

McSwite, O.C. (1997) *Legitimacy in Public Administration: a Discourse Analysis*. London: Sage.

Miliband, R. (1969) *The State in Capitalist Society*. London: Weidenfeld & Nicolson.

Miliband, R. (1973) *The State in Capitalist Society*. London: Quartet Books.

Mill, J.S. (1861/1998) *Utilitarianism*. Edited with an introduction by R. Crisp. Oxford: Oxford University Press.

Miller, D. and Dinan, W. (2008) *A Century of Spin: How Public Relations Became the Cutting Edge of Corporate Power*. London: Pluto Press.

Miller, D. and Mooney, G. (2010) Introduction to the Themed Issue. Corporate Power: Agency, Communication, Influence and Social Policy. *Critical Social Policy*, 30(4): 459–71.

Morgan, G. (2006) *Images of Organisation*. London: Sage.

Murray, C. (1984) *Losing Ground*. New York: Basic Books.

Murray, C. (1988) *In Pursuit of Happiness and Good Government*. New York: Touchstone Books.

Naim, M. (2004) From Normalcy to Lunacy. *Foreign Policy*, 141: 104.

Nelson, T.E., Clawson, R.A. and Oxley, Z.M. (1997) Media Framing of Civil Liberties Conflict and Its Effects on Tolerance. *American Political Science Review*, 91(3): 567–83.

Newman, J. (2012) *Working the Spaces of Power*. London: Bloomsbury Academic Press.

O'Connor, A. (2001) *Poverty Knowledge: Social Science, Social Policy, and the Poor in Twentieth-Century US History*. Princeton NJ: Princeton University Press.

O'Connor, J. (1973) *The Fiscal Crisis of the State*. New York: St Martin's Press.

Oliver, M. (1990) *The Politics of Disablement*. Basingstoke: Macmillan.

Olsson, J. and Hysing, E. (2012) Theorising Inside Activism: Understanding Policy Making and Policy Change from Below. *Planning Theory and Practice*, 13(2): 257–73.

Palley, E. (2012) Expected Struggles: U.S. Child Care Policy. *Children and Youth Services Review*, 34(4): 628–38.

Pinker, R.A. (1971) *Social Theory and Social Policy*. London: Heinemann.

Pinker, R.A. (1979) *The Idea of Welfare*. London: Heinemann.

Pinker, R.A. (1992) Making Sense of the Mixed Economy of Welfare. *Social Policy and Administration*, 26(4): 273–84.

Piven, F.F. (2008) *Challenging Authority: How Ordinary People Change America*. Lanham, MD: Rowman & Littlefield.

Polsby, N. (1980) *Community Power and Political Theory*. New Haven, CT: Yale University Press.

Popper, K. (1972) *The Logic of Scientific Discovery*. London: Hutchinson.

Pritchard, D. (2006) *What Is This Thing Called Knowledge?* London: Routledge.

Rai, M. and Cottle, S. (2007) Global Mediations: On the Changing Ecology of Satellite Television News. *Global Media and Communication*, 3(1): 51–78.

Rawls, J. (1993) *Political Liberalism*. New York: Columbia University Press.

Rawls, J. (1999) *A Theory of Justice*. Oxford: Oxford University Press.

Rein, M. and Schon, D. (1993) Reframing Policy Discourse, in Fischer, F. and Forester, J. (eds) *The Argumentative Turn in Policy Analysis and Planning.* Oxford: Oxford University Press, pp 145–66.

Reinsborough, P. and Canning, D. (2010) *Reimagining Change.* Oakland, CA: PM Press.

Rhodes, M.L. (1986) *Ethical Dilemmas in Social Service.* Boston, MA: Routledge and Kegan Paul.

Rich, A. (1980) Compulsory Heterosexuality and Lesbian Existence. *Signs: Journal of Women in Culture and Society*, 5(4): 631–60.

Robinson, S.E. (2004) Punctuated Equilibrium, Bureaucratization, and Budgetary Change in Schools. *Policy Studies Journal*, 32: 25 – 39.

Ronconi, L. and Franceschelli, I. (2007) Clientelism, Public Workfare and the Emergence of the Piqueteros in Argentina, in Dinello, M. and Popov, V. (eds) *Political Institutions and Development: Failed Expectations and Renewed Hopes.* Cheltenham: Edward Elgar.

Rose, H. (1981) Rereading Titmuss: The Sexual Division of Welfare. *Journal of Social Policy*, 10(4): 477–501.

Rosenau, P.M. (1992) *Post-Modernism and the Social Sciences: Insights, Inroads and Intrusions.* Princeton, NJ: Princeton University Press.

Royal Commission for the Care and Control of the Feeble-Minded (1908) *Report Of The Royal Commission On The Care And Control Of The Feeble-minded.* London: HMSO.

Sabatier, P.A. (ed.) (1999) *Theories of the Policy Process: Theoretical Lenses on Public Policy.* Boulder, CO: Westview Press.

Sabatier, P.A. and Jenkins-Smith, H.C. (eds) (1993) *Policy Change and Learning. An Advocacy Coalition Framework.* Oxford: Westview Press.

Said, E. (1979) *Orientalism.* New York: Vintage.

Sandel, M. (2010) *Justice: What's the Right Thing to Do?* London: Penguin.

Saul, D. (2009) *Campaign! Make an Impact.* London: British Library.

Scalmer, S. (2002) *Dissent Events: Protest, the Media and the Political Gimmick in Australia.* Kensington: University of New South Wales Press.

Schattschneider, E.E. (1960) *The Semisovereign People: A Realist's View of Democracy in America.* Hinsdale, IL: Dryden Press.

Schram, S.E. (1995) *Words of Welfare. The Poverty of Social Science and the Social Science of Poverty.* Minneapolis, MN: University of Minneapolis Press.

Scott, J.C. (1990) *Domination and the Arts of Resistance: Hidden Transcripts.* New Haven, CT: Yale University Press.

Sharpe, L.J. (1975) The Social Scientist and Policy Making: Some Cautionary Thoughts and Transatlantic Reflections. *Policy and Politics*, 4(2): 7–34.

Shepherd, P.L. (1985) Transnational Corporations and the International Cigarette Industry, in Newfarmer, R.S. (ed) *Profits Progress and Poverty: Case Studies of International Industries in Latin America.* Notre Dame: University of Notre Dame Press.

Shore, C. and Wright, S. (eds) (1997) *Anthropology of Policy: Critical Perspectives on Governance and Power.* New York: Routledge.

Silver, H. (1994) Social Exclusion and Social Solidarity: Three Paradigms. *International Labour Review*, 133: 531–78.

Silverman, D. (1985) *Qualitative Methodology and Sociology.* Aldershot: Gower.

Simmons, H.G. (1978) Explaining Social Policy: The English Mental Deficiency Act of 1913. *Journal of Social History*, 11(3): 387–403.

Simon, H.A. (1953) Notes on the Observation and Measurement of Political Power. *Journal of Politics*, 15: 500–16.

Simon, H.A. (1957) *Administrative Behaviour*, 2nd edn. New York: Free Press.

Simpson, G. and Connor, S. (2011) *Social Policy for Social Welfare Professionals.* Bristol: Policy Press.

Sitrin, M. (2006) *Horizontalism: Voices of Popular Power in Argentina.* Oakland, CA and Edinburgh: AK Press.

Skocpol, T. (1988) The Limits of the New Deal System and the Roots of Contemporary Welfare Dilemmas, in Weir, M., Orloff, A.S. and Skocpol, T. (eds) *The Politics of Social Policy in the United States.* Princeton, NJ: Princeton University Press, pp 293–311.

Smith, J. (1983) Quantitative vs. Interpretative: The Problem of Conducting Social Inquiry, in House, E. (ed) *Philosophy of Evaluation.* San Francisco, CA: Jossey Bass.

Spencer, H. (1898) *The Principles of Biology*, vol 1. London: Williams and Norgate.

Spencer, H. (1898) *The Principles of Biology*, vol 2. London: Williams and Norgate.

Spicker, P. (2006) *Policy Analysis for Practice: Applying Social Policy.* Bristol: Policy Press.

Spicker, P. (2011) Generalisation and Phronesis: Rethinking the Methodology of Social Policy. *Journal of Social Policy*, 40(1): 1–19.

Spicker, P. (2013) *Reclaiming Individualism: Perspectives on Individualism.* Bristol: Policy Press.

Spivak, G. (1988) Can the Subaltern Speak? in Nelson, C. and Grossberg, L. (eds) *Marxism and the Interpretation of Culture.* Urbana, IL: University of Illinois Press, pp. 271–313.

Starke, P., Kaasch, A. and van Hooren, F. (2011) *Explaining the Variety of Social Policy Responses to Economic Crisis: How Parties and Welfare State Structures Interact.* TranState working papers, No. 154.

Stedman-Jones, G. (1984) *Outcast London: A Study in the Relationship between Social Classes in Victorian Society.* Harmondsworth: Penguin.

Steensland, B. (2008) *The Failed Welfare Revolution: America's Struggle Over Guaranteed Income Policy.* Princeton, NJ: Princeton University Press.

Stone, D.A. (1989) Causal Stories and the Formation of Policy Agendas. *Political Science Quarterly*, 104(2): 281–300.

Strauss, A. and Corbin, J. (1990) *Basics of Qualitative Research.* Newbury Park, CA: Sage.

Strauss, A. and Corbin, J. (1994) Grounded Theory Methodology, in Denzin, N.K. and Lincoln, Y.S. (eds), *Handbook of Qualitative Research.* Thousand Oaks, CA: Sage.

Sum, N.-L. (2009) The Production of Hegemonic Policy Discourses: Competitiveness as a Knowledge Brand and Its (Re) Contextualisations. *Critical Policy Studies*, 3(2): 184–203.

Taylor, M. (2003) *Public Policy in the Community.* Basingstoke: Palgrave.

TFK (2007) *Campaign Contributions by Tobacco Interests: Annual Report.*

Tobacco Free Kids Action Fund / Common Cause.

Thompson, J.B. (1995) *The Media and Modernity: A Social Theory of the Media*. Cambridge: Polity Press.

Thomson, M. (1998) *The Problem of Mental Deficiency: Eugenics, Democracy and Social Policy in Britain, c. 1870–1959*. Oxford: Clarendon.

Tilly, C. (2005) *Popular Contention in Great Britain, 1758–1834*. Boulder, CO: Paradigm.

Titmuss, R.M. (1958) *Essays on the Welfare State*. London: Allen and Unwin.

Vaara, E. and Tiernari, J. (2008) A Discursive Perspective on Legitimation Strategies in Multinational Corporations. *Academy of Management Review*, 33(4): 985–93.

Van Aelst, P. and Walgrave, S. (2004) New Media, New Movements? The Role of the Internet in Shaping the 'Anti-Globalization' Movement, in van de Donk, W., Loader, B., Nixon, P.G. and Dieter, D. (eds) *Cyberprotest*. London: Routledge.

van Dijk, T.A. (1993) Principles of Critical Discourse Analysis. *Discourse & Society*, 4(2): 249–83.

van Dijk, T.A. (1998) *Ideology: A Multidisciplinary Approach*. London: Sage.

van Leeuwen, T. (2005) *Introducing Social Semiotics*. London: Routledge.

van Leeuwen, T. (2007) Legitimacy in Discourse and Communication. *Discourse and Communication*, 1(1): 91–112.

van Leeuwen, T. and Wodak, R. (1999) Legitimizing Immigration Control: A Discourse Historical Analysis. *Discourse Studies*, 1(1): 83–118.

van Zwanenberg, P. and Millstone, E. (2003) BSE: A Paradigm of Policy Failure. *The Political Quarterly*, 74 (1): 27–37.

Vardy, P. and Grosch, P. (1999) *The Puzzle of Ethics*. London: Fount.

Vestergaard, A. (2008) Branding the Humanitarian: The case of Amnesty International. *Journal of Language and Politics*, 7(3): 471–93.

Walgrave, S. and Manssens, J. (2000) The Making of the White March: The Mass Media as a Mobilizing Alternative to Movement Organizations. *Mobilization*, 5(2): 217–39.

Walt, G., Shiffman, J., Schneider, H., Murray, S.F., Brugha, R. and Gilson, L. (2008) Doing Health Policy Analysis: Methodological and Conceptual Reflections and Challenges. *Health Policy and Planning*, 23(5): 308–17.

Warner, M. (1991) Introduction: Fear of a Queer Planet. *Social Text*, 29: 3–17

Weber, M. (1964) *The Theory of Social and Economic Organisation*. New York: The Free Press.

Weiss, J.A. (1989) The Powers of Problem Definition: the Case of Government Paperwork. *Policy Sciences*, 22(2): 97–121.

Welshman, J. (2006) *Underclass: A History of the Excluded, 1880–2000*. London: Hambledon Continuum.

Wenden, A. (2005) The Politics of Representation: A Critical Discourse Analysis of an Al Jazeera Special Report. *International Journal of Peace Studies*, 10(2): 89–112.

White, A. (1885) The Nomad of Poor London. *Contemporary Review*, 47: 714–26.

White, A. (1901/1973) *Efficiency and Empire*. Edited and with an introduction and notes by G.R. Searle. Brighton: Harvester Press.

Whitelaw, A. and Williams, J. (1994) Relating Health Education Research

172 WHAT'S YOUR PROBLEM?

to Health Policy. *Health Education Research*, 9(4): 519–26.

Wildavsky, A. (1980) *Speaking Truth to Power: The Art and Craft of Policy Analysis*. London: Macmillan.

Williams, F. (1989) *Social Policy: A Critical Introduction – Issues of Race, Gender and Class*. Cambridge: Polity.

Wodak, R. and Ludwig, C. (eds) (1999) *Challenges in a Changing World: Issues in Critical Discourse Analysis*. Vienna: Passagenverlag.

Wohl, A.S. (1968) The Bitter Cry of Outcast London. *International Review of Social History*, 12(2): 189–245.

Wolff, J. (2007) (De)Mobilising the Marginalised: A Comparison of the Argentine Piqueteros and Ecuador's Indigenous Movement. *Journal of Latin American Studies*, 39: 1–29.

Wood, G. (1985) The Politics of Development Policy Labelling. *Development and Change*, 16: 347–73.

Wootliff, J. and Deri, C. (2001) NGOs: The New Super Brands. *Corporate Reputation Review*, 4(2): 157–66.

World Health Organization (2003) *World Health Organization Framework Convention on Tobacco Control*. Geneva, Switzerland: World Health Organization.

World Health Organization (2011) *World Health Organization Report on the Global Tobacco Epidemic*. Geneva, Switzerland: World Health Organization.

World Health Organization (2012a) *Tobacco Industry Interference: A Global Brief*. Geneva, Switzerland: World Health Organization.

World Health Organization (2012b) *Confronting the Tobacco Epidemic in a New Era of Trade and Investment Liberalization*. Geneva, Switzerland: World Health Organization.

Wright Mills, C. (1963) *Power, Politics and People. The Collected Essays of C. Wright Mills*. Edited by Irving H. Horowitz. New York: Oxford University Press.

Yanow, D. (1996) *How Does a Policy Mean? Interpreting Policy and Organizational Actions*. Washington: George University Press.

Yanow, D. (2010) Interpretation in Policy Analysis: On Methods and Practice. *Critical Policy Studies*, 1(1): 110–22.

Index